Amalfi Blue

lost & found in the south of Italy

by

Lisa Fantino

First Edition
Published by
Wanderlust Women Travel Ltd.
424 Mamaroneck Avenue
Mamaroneck, NY 10543
Visit our website at:
www.WanderlustWomenTravel.com

Cover design & all photos by Lisa Fantino
Author photo by Rochelle Cheever

ISBN: 0988496917
ISBN-13: 978-0-9884969-1-0

Library of Congress
LCCN: 2012951858

Dedication

This book is dedicated to the three people who inspired me to write my story.

To my Mom, Teri Fantino, first and always for giving me wings and supporting each and every romantic notion that I have ever had.

To my Dad, Alfred Fantino, who held my feet to the ground, even when Mom encouraged me to fly.

To Rocco, who breathed life into my tired soul and continues to inspire me daily.

Ti voglio bene sai.

Special Thanks

There are many people I have met along the way. Many of them are mentioned throughout this journey while others need to be recognized here.

Tops on the list are: Bob Guccione, Jr., my writing and publishing hero. I thank you for your support and friendship and editorial suggestions along the way. Maybe one day when we're in those rockers at Shady Pines you'll explain why you never hired me;

Sonia Hall for encouraging me to go clear my head in a land that I have grown to love;

Susan Segal for years of friendship and for always and graciously opening your home to me;

My good friend and beautiful photographer, Rochelle Cheever; and my talented videographer, Chris Saave.

Contents

Prelude

Prelude

Today is Tuesday April 3, 2012. It's my third day here and it's a bit isolating and lonely. The apartment is lovely and I can stare out my window at yards of lemon and orange groves but I don't know a soul except business contacts.

When I'm on the street, I look at each passing car in hopes...or fear...of seeing him everywhere I go. This place...traveling the world...has always been about him, for the past four years, and now it's not and that's very lonely.

My apartment is a dream. I should be dancing on clouds inside this magnificent villa; yet, it's the cloud of us together which colors my days and looms at night.

I wake each morning hoping today will be the day I see him drive by on a *moto*, expecting to see him in the piazza, longing to share this apartment with him each night. I was lonely in New York but here it is loneliness coupled with isolation.

Living in a foreign country is always isolating at first, especially when you don't know a soul. It's the start of a new adventure and I hope that these empty feelings pass sooner rather than later. I have my life to live.

Chapter 1 - The Journey Begins

ove defines us be it good or bad. It is what breathes life into us from the moment we take our first breath. Without it, babies do not develop properly and without it, adults become lifeless. It courses through our being, physically, emotionally and psychically. Yes, I said psychically, not psychologically, although it does that as well.

Love is the start and the end of all significant journeys in our life and this is where my current story begins, for it is the love of a daughter and father which lead me to the Amalfi Coast for the first time four years ago.

It is for the love of a man that I also fell in love with a place. It is for that same love that makes me return each year and brings me here now to start my new adventure, the next chapter, to borrow a well-worn phrase.

I lost my Dad six years ago, after a long, grueling battle with Alzheimer's disease. It was his battle but as his primary caregiver for nearly six years, it was a battle I fought with him each and every day. His was not the same battle as had previously claimed his two sisters. They suffered severe dementia. Dad suffered dementia, eventually, but Alzheimer's hit him hardest in the frontal and parietal lobes of his brain, effecting judgment and motor coordination.

That was hardest for him because he was an architect and an amazing artist. He would cut his steak into equal bite-sized pieces without realizing it. He could build anything without measuring; yet, his rule was always measure twice and cut once. So, when Dad first started showing symptoms, it was his driving and coordination which faltered. Then he couldn't measure a job site and draw plans. It was the beginning of the end of life as my family knew it.

This is not about my Dad's journey but serves as the prelude to my arrival at this moment in time. You see, Italian-American fathers and daughters have a love like no other. As girls, they cherish and protect us but they also teach us to be independent and strong. We are at once their princess and their shortstop. I can act like a lady and hit one out of the park at softball.

When you lose that first, strong, male love in your life, a part of your soul dies. When you see those you have always looked to for strength suddenly powerless, it leaves you feeling lost. What is placed before us is challenging and it can either destroy us or empower us to rise to new levels.

So much of me had been tied to taking care of my Dad for more than six years that I no longer nurtured myself. I rebounded by taking a long-held dream trip to Athens to climb the Acropolis and with a bad relationship with a man I gave too much importance to in a failed attempt to fill that void of male energy in my life.

Fast forward two years. After settling the estate with my sisters, I set out to Italy to find me again!

I have always flown solo in many ways but especially in travel. I get my fierce sense of independence from my Mom, who was a single mother, and my Dad who taught me many father-son bonding skills since he had no male off-spring. So, on the heels of a great sense of loss and stress in my life, I yearned for a solo escape to center myself again.

Enter a friend I had not seen in a good ten years and someone with whom I had never traveled. This should have

3

been the first red flag! You should never travel with some- one for the first time on a trip which needs to be about you.

She asked to come along, saying she would join me in Rome. Noticing my reluctance, she also insisted that she would be the easiest travel companion ever! Second red flag! You don't know someone until you live or travel with them.

I flew in from New York; she journeyed from Paris and by the time we arrived at our hotel in Rome, her diva skills were in full swing. She much preferred drinking in the hotel bar than exploring the Eternal City in the rain. Oh Lord, how do I get myself into these things? Third red flag!

This was definitely not the relaxing journey my heart and soul craved for, not to mention my stressed and taut body!

It rained, it poured, she snored and I could not wait to head south, having now booked my own room in Sorrento one late night from the computer in the hotel lobby. I was sure the Amalfi Coast would be my reward after entertain- ing her for three days. Yet, she was not the worst of it...I was nearly kidnapped.

There are two statues which sit in my bathroom. My favorite is Cupid's complete rapture of Psyche. As she gazes at him adoringly, trusting in that first blush of love, he is about to lift her in his winged arms and carry her to bliss. Yeah, we all dream of that, right? Well, it could happen.

The other is of a reclining Pauline Bonaparte, which is so me, for anyone who truly knows me. Both are by the wonderful neo-classical, Italian sculptor, Antonio Canova. Anyway, I had asked *La Principessa* if she wanted to join me in visiting *Villa Borghese* because the original reclining Pauline by Canova was on display. *Certo*! She was supposed to give me the 25 bucks for the ticket when we got to Italy. Yeah, I'm still waiting on that!

Anyway, this lovely, sunny day I headed out for *Villa Borghese*, again alone but armed with an extra ticket. I asked three very helpful Italians and two not so helpful bus monitors in Piazza Venezia where to catch Bus #9. They all provided detailed instructions on how to get to the bus stop, which I was apparently directly across from and which was within my sightline.

I strolled across the Piazza to Via della Teatro Marcello, searching for the bus that was never coming.

"*Signora, bisogna aiuta? Dov'è vuoi andare?*" A charming voice asked pleasantly.

I turned to see a well-dressed man with salt and pepper hair, sparkling blue eyes and a cheerful smile.

5

"*Parlo italiano un po*," I say, proud of my ability to respond with that much.

"No, you must be Italian, *faccia bella italiana*, and those eyes," *Mamma mia*, he was a bilingual flirt.

Even though I let my NYC guard down while on vacation, post-911, I am more cautious. Yet, when this Lothario offered to drive me to *Villa Borghese*, I went freely. After all, he was well-dressed and his rental car was parked at the bus stop. I thought it was highly doubtful that he was stalking stupid tourists all day. Another one of those damn red flags.

Off we go to visit Pauline Bonaparte and I learn that Nico is a veterinarian who lives with his big dog and mamma in Firenze. What else? This guy was just shy of 50 and with a professed career. Are they all *mammones* here?

En route, he also insists that we have dinner and invites me to Firenze because this was *Weekend di Pasqua* and I should spend it with Nico e mamma, *certo*.

"You can see your friends anytime but we have only just met."

Oh, Dio, they come out of the womb flirting and possessive. I truly believe that when God sees the storks with baby boys heading to Earth, he sprinkles extra flirting DNA on the bundles headed to the boot of Italy.

I laugh it off and since Mom always told me, *uno mano lave l'altra*, I offer him *La Principessa's* "free" ticket to join me. He jumps at the chance to grab my arm and we go off skipping into the Villa for a few laughs. Seriously, we were skipping. How dangerous could this be?

Then, just like that, there it is - Canova's vision of a reclining lady. I fantasize that some muscular house boy has just peeled her a few grapes and she devoured him. I want that; I need that; damn, I vow to be raptured on this trip...but certainly not by Nico, the crazed vet.

He offers to drive to Castello Gandolfo and I figure, why not? The only thing waiting for me at the hotel is someone who doesn't want to do anything. This is a no-brainer!

Only I forget that this is Good Friday in Rome. I can only imagine that this is what it was like when the Jews made the mass Exodus. The roads at 4 o 'clock make Manhattan rush hour look like a leisurely Sunday drive. It's automotive insanity, Italian style.

I insist we head back because I need to get away from this guy and that's when it takes a turn for the worse. He turns on a euro. We are on a six lane road, three each way, and he does a 180. OK, this was not in my guidebook. The reporter in me starts scoping out landmarks and praying

7

that the bumper to bumper traffic continues in case I need to jump from his moving rental car. I even look out the car window, trying to catch the eye of a passing motorist with a look of desperation.

Come si dice "SOS" in italiano?

Ahead, there are signs for Firenze to the right and Roma to the left. Naturally, we are far right and I keep insisting that he move over. The tension is mounting exponentially along with the increase in traffic, until 100 feet short of the turnoff, where he cuts across three lanes of traffic. In one slick hair-raising turn, we are now heading to Rome.

Stay focused, Lisa, he is at least going in the right direction. The silence is deafening and I now realize that I do not have my cell phone with me and no one knows where I am. This damn red flag now becomes an internal SOS beacon.

Fortunately, I never told him the name of my hotel, only the nearest monument, where he drops me. The literal icing on the cake happens as I step out of his car and a pigeon poops on my head and my new black suede jacket. I look up and pray to *Nonna*, "*There had better be a reward waiting for me on the Amalfi Coast.*" Little did I know how my life was about to change forever.

Chapter 2 - For the Love of a Man

With *La Principessa* as my co-pilot, we high-tailed it out of Rome before the crazed vet returned. My neck tensed as I seemed to drive in endless circles trying to find the elusive Autostrada, which I could see in the distance, but neither I nor my GPS could seem to find the entrance ramp.

The gloom and grey of another rainy day in Rome seemed to trap us like a net as *motos* whizzed by and horns flared. Downtown traffic is the same across the globe and just as stressful. However, we were in a Benz, built like a tank, and armed with a military determination to escape to sunnier climates.

Once on the highway, I could feel the stress leave my body at 130 kilometers per hour. The road opened before me and behind the wheel of my black luxury sedan, I felt like a new woman. The further we journeyed from Rome, the more that knot in the back of my neck relaxed. This was not where I was born but I was certain that I was home.

All road signs here headed for Napoli and so were we. We exited the highway in *Castellammare di Stabia*, a ship-building port with the biggest Bingo hall outside of Vegas. It was not the prettiest part of Napoli and certainly it did not look like the safest.

This was *Pasquetta*, the Monday after Easter, and everything seemed closed. Metal gates were down. Shop lights were out. We worried that we came during an off-season holiday break.

We passed through *Vico Equense* and *Meta* and the rugged coastal beauty began to reveal itself slowly, around each twist and turn. The sun came out, a refreshing change after rain-soaked Rome. The beauty was overwhelming as an azure sea kissed a turquoise sky so that we could not distinguish where one ended and the other began and this truly was just the beginning.

I immersed myself in the history of the Amalfi region before leaving New York and the archaeology of Campania was a must-see on this journey. Visiting the ruins at *Pompei* and *Herculaneum*, again alone, would be where history would come alive for me.

As a child, I remembered learning of the devastation at Pompei but as an adult I was astonished when they discovered hundreds of carbonized skeletons huddled in boathouses in *Ercolano* in the late 1980s and early 90s. Mothers died sheltering children with their bodies. Men died with looks of true anguish on their faces. These images haunted me.

The romantic in me, yes, I am, if you couldn't guess that by my expressed desire to be raptured and flown away, dreamed of life in Herculaneum, modern day Ercolano. Here is where the upper class vacationed. Here is where ancient villas were preserved as if their inhabitants went out for lunch at *una tavola calda*. Here is where I yearned to visit and I did…again in the rain, *piove, piove e piove più*!

The day trips were the perfect buffer from the stress of the city I left behind in the States and Rome to the transition to Sorrento. For me, this was not just a change in geography and time zones but more like a modulation from insanity to serenity. I seemed to be relaxing for the first time in years.

Stress takes on a different face when you are surrounded by natural beauty. The people of this region struggle with the economic crisis on a daily basis but at their core, *in loro cuori e anime*, they truly let go and let God give them strength. Stress-relief comes in the form of three-hour lunch breaks, whether to eat or to make love; after all, this is Italy.

I strolled through the villages, visiting the beach in *Minori*, where the waterfront promenade reminded me of *Nonna's* old haunt, Hollywood, Florida. I enjoyed an afternoon *aperitivo* or espresso in Sorrento's Fauno Bar while thinking where to explore next.

Driving *La Costiera Amalfitana* became a welcome escape on a daily basis, stopping at each overlook, where possible, or grabbing a curb for the perfect photo op. Time didn't matter here. I left time behind.

Tension with *La Principessa* was less now that we had separate rooms and I insisted on separate dinner checks as well. Sleeping alone is always preferable to sleeping with the wrong person...even when they're not a lover.

The spring rains finally gave way to sun and I was determined to take the ferry to *Capri* and explore *Grotta Azzurra*, the famed Blue Grotto where Emperor Tiberius reportedly swam.

I walked the long cliff drop down to the Marina Piccola in Sorrento to catch the hydrofoil to Capri. There was no hurry. If I missed the first boat, another would be along in 30 minutes. Dozens of people came aboard. It was the first sunny day after what had seemed like weeks of rain. True, it was the calming effect of the sea that I sought but when you are surrounded by loud tourists, screaming children and the constant drone of the boat's engines, it's hard to relax.

The Grotto is only open weather-permitting because you enter the cave through a two-foot tall opening in a tiny row boat. Rough seas can make the task quite treacherous and I was happy the sun made the trip possible this day.

Landing on this, the isle of the gods, you must take two additional smaller boats to reach the famed Grotto. The second row boat is a trip and a half, as some 15 to 20 people are squished like *alici* in a can. We are instructed by the boatman, in Italian, *certo*, to lie down, on top of each other, in order to enter the Grotto. I see the two-foot tall opening ahead of us and think this bobbing dinghy is never going to make it. Did someone say claustrophobia?

And there I go, flat back with my head in the crotch of a septuagenarian I had only just met. Needless to say, he truly enjoyed his journey into the unknown, as the boatman crouched, so as not to bang his head along the jagged cave entrance.

Inside the Grotto, a natural phenomenon with the sun makes the water glow an iridescent blue under the water of the darkened cave. Yet, a dozen tiny row boats circling inside make it look like *Circo Massimo* at rush hour.

Enough with the huddled masses. I needed to explore Capri on my own, in the sun, and be swept away.

A cable car carried me to what seemed liked the tip of heaven. One step off the *funicolare* and my blood pressure dropped further - not in the bad, you're going to die way, but in the fantasmic you have just come alive way. The heady scent of wisteria mixed with jasmine and beckoned me to stroll along the coast toward the *Faraglioni*.

The higher I climbed and strolled, off the beaten path, the further behind I left civilization. I walked and climbed and walked some more, hoping to put the past behind me, until happening upon Via Tragara.

A small sign, grounded to an old stone wall, mentioned poet Pablo Neruda, who had spent many fruitful years in this paradise, writing of love's rapture. Here it was easy for me to understand the inspiration for the poet's verses of love: "*...everything carries me to you, as if everything that exists, aromas, light, metals, were little boats that sail toward those isles of yours that wait for me.*" Capri, this day, this moment, was heaven-sent and would come to an end all too quickly.

I made my way back to the dock for the short ferry ride back to Sorrento, not knowing that my life would change in an instant. I hadn't noticed him before, maybe the crowd had obscured my view or perhaps I just wasn't ready for him. As I neared the dock, the first to arrive, there he stood, like the sun-tanned descendant of Apollo himself, hotter than the white sands of an east coast beach and disarmingly appealing.

"So, you like Capri?" He asked in the sexiest accent imaginable. He stood waiting for me at the end of the dock to welcome me onboard. His dark eyes peered over his black sunglasses like deep pools of liquid chocolate, melting my veneer.

The smiles were brief. The greetings exchanged in two languages but it was the silent discourse that resonated between us and the ferry crowd melted away into the Bay of Naples. He asked me to salsa and right then and there no one else mattered. No one else was there. We danced on deck as if no one was watching. I finally knew what that saying meant. I finally knew where I belonged.

I came alive again that night. What girl wouldn't when given the dinner choice between *Positano* or *Pompei* with tall, dark and oh my God? Was this my life? Yes and I was being rewarded as I had prayed and as the angels had listened from above. *Grazie tante, Nonna.*

15

Rocco breathed fire into my soul again. Fireworks lit the night sky over Pompei, as we rounded the bend. OK, so there are fireworks in Naples almost every night but this was my night.

"I did this for you," he laughed and I didn't care because the gesture was romantic and genuine. Passion in the back of an old Lancia, off the side of the road, until bright lights approached us from the rear.

Polizia, mamma mia, and again we were both 17.

"Documenti?"

The officers asked for our documents, as if we were in some World War II film noir. I was in the car laughing hysterically while Rocco listened to their warnings of highwaymen with *pistola* and that this was not a safe place for us to enjoy *l'amore*. The visit from the *polizia* only added to the rapture and excitement of *una bella notte*.

The evening ended in the morning and all too quickly because I was set to return to Rome in four hours.

We kept in touch with the occasional SMS. He eventually found a girlfriend and I was some 4,400 miles away, give or take a hundred. I never imagined that we would go any further. He would remain my forever fantasy come to life. Yet, when I left that day, I knew I would return for *Capodanno*, the Italian New Years Eve.

Mom always said that how you start the New Year will be how you finish it and I wanted to start and end it over the Bay of Naples.

However, my life was about to change again in a shattering event for my best friend.

Chapter 3 - As Only a Mother Can

*I*t was a lazy September morning. The sun was out and the end of summer was drawing near. The only decision of the day was whether to take the usual Saturday ride to upstate New York, antiquing with Mom.

I started the morning Skype-chatting with my friend Maurizio. Modern technology makes the world a very small place, as I sat in New York listening to him on headsets in Torino, with the birds chirping outside my window.

I didn't know where Mom was, even though we often spent Saturdays together. It was our routine to check in with each other after she made her bagel run and I rolled out of bed but this Saturday was different. She hadn't answered the phone by noon, so I thought she had plans.

In my entire life, Mom was the one person I could count on, always. She was and still is part parent, cheerleader, confidante, best friend and sometimes, even partner in crime. After all, how many mothers would stop Jon Bon Jovi in his tracks on Chicago's tony Michigan Avenue, holding him in conversation, until I could catch up to say hello. Or insist in a Big Apple recording studio that another rocker kiss me for a unique photo op?

Mom was and is part rocker and part anchor and if you are to understand how my life changed forever that September morning, then, you need to know my Mom.

After my parents' divorce, my Mom became my super-hero. There was no building she could not scale, no rock club she would not go to, no fire she would not walk through for me and my sister. If we were happy, she was happy. If we were hurt, she would make it all better, whether we were one or 41 and whether it was 1:00 pm or 1:00 am.

So, while I had not yet heard from her this day, I was hardly worried, when my world came crashing down around me in a short five-minute period.

A call from a hospital E.R. nurse told me that my Mom had a stroke while driving.

"She is awake and talking but you need to get here as soon as possible."

Suddenly, all of the pieces started to fit. The scenes which puzzled me for the past few months played in my mind, over and over, and started to come together.

There were a number of times that her legs had buckled when stepping off a curb. Then there were the times that she had forgotten something which she had done numerous times before. This wasn't dementia. I knew what that was, several times over by now, having cared for my aunt and Dad. No, what Mom had was neurological and as the year wound down, she promised me that she would get medical insurance in the New Year. Yet, waiting nearly killed her.

The diagnosis was a severe hemorrhagic stroke on the right side of the brain, affecting her judgment and leaving left side weakness and a speech deficit. It was a grueling six months in nursing homes and the 24/7 care of my sister and I, who were her biggest cheerleaders, because she had always been ours.

"This couldn't be happening again," I thought. She was my Mom. She had been my strong shoulder when Dad was sick and dying. She had been there for each and every heartbreak that I had ever suffered. She sat through law school orientation for significant others to understand how my behavior would change in the process and supported me during that four year marathon. She was the one person who taught me to never to give up on blissful romance. Now, I had to be her voice and also her caregiver, again!

Three months into the third rehab center and New Years Eve was fast approaching. I talked with Mom about the New Years' trip prior to her stroke but didn't dare ask whether I should leave her side now. Then, in a way only a mother can, she asked me.

"Look around. I have more nurses looking at me than I know what to do with," she insisted. "Nothing is going to happen to me that hasn't happened already."

She assured me that she was well cared for and would still be there when I returned.

"Call Rocco. See what he says," and that was all it took, a suggestion from Mom.

I texted him that I would be in Sorrento.

"Where will you be for *Capodanno*?" I asked, not knowing what to expect.

"Wherever you are," was the reply I quickly received.

Chapter 4 - Losing My Heart

Sono molto felice tu sei in Sorrento was the text waiting for me as soon as the captain told us we could turn on our phones. Rocco said we'd have dinner somewhere, although he hadn't had time to make reservations. Typical Italian event planning!

He had worked on the ferry late that night so I figured we were going somewhere casual. When he called me from the lobby, I ran down barely able to contain myself. To my total delight and surprise, there he stood in an ash grey tux with a present for me, while there I stood in a tunic sweater and leggings. We both giggled and I ran up to my room and hurried into my bangled, little black dress.

"How did you remember me?" he asked, sweeping me up for a giant embrace.

Was he kidding? Sure, it had been nine months but some things you never forget. I mean, does he not look in the mirror to shave? Does he not see what I see?

We were on fire that night. We headed down the pitch black Amalfi Drive, lit only by the Naples skyline and the fairytale, candlelit *presepi*, placed lovingly by locals into the cliffside. He was my Prince Charming and this night was magic.

Giggles mixed with kisses were the soundtrack for our long drive in search of a place to eat. The black of the night sky and the stars above gave us a false sense of security in that one wrong kiss would have us soaring off the edge and into the sea below.

After driving for more than an hour, we realized that any futile effort now to reach the romantic, medieval Torre Normana in *Maiori* would not let us return to the hotel terrace for fireworks in time for *mezzanotte*.

Here we were, ready for the red carpet, and we stopped for dinner at the last tiny restaurant open for the evening in *Minori*. It was wonderful and we never noticed that the people at the only other occupied table were dressed in jeans.

The return trip was full of more stolen kisses in the dark. Hands sliding cautiously around each other and the hairpin turns but I persevered and *mezzanotte* was well worth the wait. *Capodanno* in Naples is unlike any pyrotechnic show staged by any professionals anywhere. It lasts more than an hour and sounds and smells like the London Blitz.

Sulfur in the air, Dom in our glasses, *ahhh, tutto romantico.*

Auguri, auguri, we shouted from the massive terrace. Wrapped in each other, we ushered in the New Year under the glowing embers of giant fireworks.

His kisses were hotter than a Roman candle. Something was suddenly different. We explored each other with a passion so real and so deep that rapture could not describe it. Our celebration lasted until we fell asleep in each other's arms, too tired for one second more of passion.

As the first dawn of a New Year peeked through the drapes, I felt him roll over me. Neither of us needed to open our eyes. Instinctively, we let our bodies see and feel their way. Each sensation was like a first kiss. Each second of this year would draw us closer together and so our three-and-a-half year romance began. Rocco and I stood between now and forever and I wanted to spend all of the moments in between with him.

We traveled the world together. Ischia, Procida, Nerano in Italy and New York, Philadelphia, Chicago, San Antonio and more in the United States. We mirrored each other's sense of wanderlust to explore each corner of the world and each other.

Our long separations fueled our hunger and each reunion was as if there was the magic of that first kiss all over again. We never fought, not once. Why waste time in life arguing over trivialities. If we could each apply that to our daily lives, just imagine how much better the art of humanity would be.

Living together was easy from the get-go. From the moment he arrived in New York for his long visits, we gave each other the space we needed to survive together. Any two people, when confined to 800 square feet, can drive each other insane but we drove each other mad with passion not frustration.

His ardor for us was matched by his fervor for food; after all, he is Italian. Rocco's smile lit up my life and the kitchen. There is nothing sexier than a man who cooks, right? Wrong, there is nothing sexier than an Italian god who cooks in his briefs and then does the dishes.

Cooking is for Rocco what writing is for me. They are the creative outlets which give us joy. They bring inspiration and provide expression for emotion, which also makes us vulnerable for sharing our innermost desires.

Mornings would start with breakfast in bed. He knew his way around the kitchen and into my heart. Dessert at night, well, dessert was the sweetest way to end our days with *sogni d'oro*. This was the easiest relationship which had ever illuminated my heart.

Yet, Rocco was gun-shy over two things - marriage and mastering English. He saw one as a doorway to prison and the other as limiting his ability to live and work in New York. He was a true Scorpio. They mull over every dark detail under a pessimistic cloud without ever seeing the light in the silver lining. Could he not understand that the true miracle was that two people could keep such honesty and passion alive over the miles and years?

It amazes me how people who truly profess to care for you under the umbrella of friendship cannot simply embrace your happiness without applying their own agenda. Not one person in my life, not one, except my Mom, could just accept the constant smile on my face and the newfound lightness of my being after such a long, tumultuous time in my life. Not one so-called friend ever made time to meet Rocco when he came to the U.S. except John. He is, was and will always be a true friend and Rocco truly appreciated meeting him.

For Rocco, there were the constant queries about why he dated an American girl, the language barrier and the age difference (it was 20 years). None of these issues mattered when we were together; yet, they became increasingly dominant during times apart. How could they not? The constant drone of anything becomes part of your psyche if applied long enough. It's like the wearing down of a prisoner of war. If someone tells you something long enough without positive reinforcement, it becomes the voice you hear, the call you answer, the bee you swat just to drown out the din.

So, it was for us. I started to give into the issues of jealousy raised by my friends who questioned the existence of other girls. Personally, the lawyer in me never asked him the question I didn't want answered. I assumed there were other girls for sex, here or there, but none of importance. After all, he was with me for three *Capodannos* and he flew across an ocean and through blizzards just to be with me. No one else mattered.

He gave into the insecurities and challenges of moving overseas and committing to one woman. What is it with Italian men? They personify and idolize Lothario. They cannot understand that the true miracle in life is finding one woman to endure your bullshit and still think you're hot in the morning.

There was so much about Rocco that was atypical of the worst in Napoletani men. He was honest, spiritual, emotional, deeply caring and passionate. Yet, when it came to commitment, he rolled back into Mamma's womb like the rest of them.

For me, I didn't care if we were married, truly, but I did want to live with him. Marriage becomes less important when you are well beyond that Cinderella age. When life's realities lay bear the fragilities of our short time here, the fairytale becomes less important than the stories shared with your leading man.

The distance was becoming more noticeable, ripples at first and then waves of emptiness. What was happening? I knew on my end that my insecurities were rearing their ugly head. The more this internal vacuum sucked at my psyche, the more he retreated. Weeks would go by without hearing a word and then months. When I finally grew strong enough to call him on Thanksgiving, hearing him say "*finisici*" was like a knife in my heart.

How does a relationship without one fight go from passionate to *finisci* in one call? Had there been someone else, had there been abuse, had there been fights or boredom or incompatibility, it would surely hurt but at least I could understand the impetus. This, this was insanity and I could not fix this, not from across an ocean. So, I set forth on my journey to find myself after losing my heart.

Chapter 5 - La Vita Bella

$\mathcal{I}$ overpacked. I was sure of it and I was much less sure whether my extra suitcase would make the connection with me through Frankfurt and onto Napoli.

Too many clothes, necessitated by the need to look drop-dead hot and for an upcoming photo shoot in Rome. Too many staples of daily living, such as spices and shampoo. Who knew what I could find and not find at a local *supermercato*.

A collapsible laundry hamper, check.

Pignoli nuts, check.

Earl Grey tea, check.

Lingerie and leather boots, check.

Winter clothes, *fuhgettaboutit*!

The journey over was simultaneously exciting and nerve-wracking. I was starting a new life in a country where

I didn't speak the local language fluently. However, I was more anxious at the lack of emotional connection with Rocco, which shook my core. He knew I was arriving but said that he didn't want to see me. That would be difficult since my new home and his parents' apartment were just blocks apart. Yes, this would be interesting.

The Villa

Orange and lemon groves lined both sides of the massive iron gates which lead to my new home, a 200-year-old villa just steps from the heart of Sorrento's Piazza Tasso. After a three month search on the Internet, I was certain I had done the right thing.

The car pulled into the driveway and the *proprietà* and her lovely daughter came out to welcome me. I was home. I knew it without stepping one foot into the marble foyer, yet, that also won me over.

I was also very glad to be away from the driver who spent the better part of an hour driving from *Capodicchino* telling me that I needed to be more like an Italian woman to make demands of Rocco. Alternatively, he stated fervently that Rocco would never leave Napoli for me. I never asked for his opinion and was so glad that my arrival in Sorrento muted his negativity.

My new landlady is adorable and tries to speak English to me, as I muddle through in my best Italian with her. Booklets for the stove and washing machine are left for me in *tutto italiano*, what else? She also gives me the keys to this castle, four of them, including a very long skeleton key which becomes my daily challenge.

I am living my dream. I have the perfect apartment, a duplex, in an Italian villa just at the end of Via degli Aranci. This is the street I had always told Rocco that I wanted to live on. So, here I sit, in the perfect apartment, in the perfect location, without the perfect man.

"Snap out of it, my dear and see how lucky you really are!"

Feeling out of sorts and out of contact with almost everything familiar, I am starting to wonder if this place will ever feel like home to me. The villa has a special warmth and it is located in my dream neighborhood but my stuff is missing.

Our life is cluttered with distractions. The distractions of work, the distractions of home, the distractions of parental responsibility all fall on our shoulders and crowd our ability to focus on who we are and what we want at our core. I would venture to say that very few of us are comfortable when those distractions are cleared away and all we are left with is ourselves.

Here I am in Italy with absolutely no distractions. My life, as I knew it, is in New York. Here, this isn't my home; yet, it gives me great comfort amid its stark surroundings. The irony is that in this secure cocoon, I am feeling very isolated, alone and depressed.

For the first time in years, maybe as long as a decade, I sit here with absolutely no direction and it's a scary place to be. I miss what I shared with Rocco. It was a soul connection. Despite the thousands of miles that separated us, there was a reason to get out of bed each morning…if only to find his daily text message.

"Buon giorno, tesoro. Sono in treno per lavoro stamattina sei stata il mio primo pensiero, tanti baci, farfallina."

Or to end the day with a smile, even though we were thousands of miles apart.

"Ciao, Dolcezza, adesso sono tornato da lavoro sto guardando le foto. Non mi stanco mai di vederle. Sei una donna speciale. Te voglio bene."

I woke up with a smile on my face to know that I shared just the simple joy of life with another person. Now that I've shared that, I'm desperate to get it back again. Yet, sitting alone in an Italian villa is not the way to make that happen.

Here there are no pictures on the walls or family photographs, no incidents of everyday life, no posters and papers with a to-do list. Here the only thing to do is focus on what I want to do and at this of stage of my life I am not sure what that is any longer.

The apartment is plain but comfortably furnished. There is no art on the walls, not even a map of Sorrento for tourists who might be here for the first time. Come to think of it, why do most houses on the Jersey Shore have a framed map on the wall? We drive there and if we haven't figured out where the Old Barnegat Lighthouse stands in relation to Exit 63, then how the hell did we arrive on Long Beach Island in the first place? Things that make you go *hmm*!

I think I have come to the realization that I do not need "stuff" to make me happy. My stuff is in New York and the only thing I truly miss is the chenille throw on the back of my chaise this cold evening. It would make for a cozy night when the *Tramontana* blow the dampness through my bones. The season has yet to change here. The cold winds of winter have yet to yield to spring.

I carry my photos in my iPad, not all of them but enough of my family and Rocco so as not to miss them. So, what would I need to make this place home to me? The answer came to me during tonight's *passeggiata*. Most of the shops had closed for the night along my stretch of Corso Italia but the florist was still open. The young girl who runs the shop seemed to be playing host to her older male relatives and she smiled just to have another woman around. I picked up a pretty pink geranium for only €4, quite sure that this would do the trick.

It was just what the doctor ordered to cure my homesickness during this Easter weekend, a garden to tend, roots to be planted, even if only on my Juliet balcony. Little did I know that it would become just as challenging as my nightly struggle with the front door lock.

Since the *Tramontana* winds blow each night, my morning chore is to upright my potted pal each morning. She is resilient, like me, putting her best face on each morning to greet the day, no matter how much she has been battered.

The morning also lays before me a path of rotting oranges and lemons, tossed about in the rough winds. There is a carpet of bruised orbs to navigate before I can make my way clear. Their sweet scent hovers on the morning dew as their tattered, wounded bodies lie exhausted, no longer able to hang onto hope.

I venture out each day looking for anyone to say, "*Yes, Lisa, you did good!*"

My challenge is the frustrating nightly battle, when I return, to tussle with the 200-year-old lock and that very long skeleton key. The rustic charm is sweet but why not update the locks? I will prevail. It is the key to my future. Sorry, I couldn't resist!

I have been here now for a week and it is simultaneously exciting and isolating. I don't have one friend, which is the lonely part, but I am discovering new ways to survive in this foreign land which is in my DNA.

I apparently share the villa with a mysterious physician. I say mysterious because he comes and goes like a cat in the night and the only evidence of his existence is the black Maserati in the driveway. Let the adventure begin!

Piano, Piano

Visiting a place and actually living there are two totally different experiences. American and British tourists come to the south of Italy and swear that the quality of life is better; yet, they are seeing it through "vacation eyes" and anywhere looks better on a holiday.

I have been a student of the Italian language, on and off, for most of my life. First it was the Sicilian and Calabrese dialects spoken in the homes of my grandparents on a daily basis and later it was the pure Roman Italian taught in adult education courses. However, getting a taste of *Napoletano* on a daily basis is an education unto itself. Words are slurred together in a spirited velocity, while large hand gestures punctuate even the smallest points.

"Piano, Piano, per favore, parlo italiano un po."

That usually gets anyone to slow down a bit but the speed soon picks up again. It's forcing me to step up my game and finally start thinking in Italian. I think that's the key to speaking any language. Don't think in your primary language and then start translating to speak. Just jump in at the deep end and start thinking like the locals.

Spero e Sogno

Amid such beauty, the spring tempest hangs, literally, like the grey cloud that it is, over the Lattari Mountains in the distance. It threatens to disrupt life in paradise. It is like life. Storms come and go and threaten our core, but it is how we deal with the gloom on the horizon that can turn it around and let the light shine through. Don't you agree?

We can recoil into a world of darkness, lolling in bed, buried under the covers, or we can toss them off and shout out, "I'm here world. Let's have at it."

I am in paradise. Granted, there isn't much to do here but gaze upon beauty, whether it's the landscape or men, but there can be worse things in life. I have decided that I will make my life change. I am tired of waiting for the clouds to break because they are in God's hands and I figure since he is a man, or at least that's what 13 years in Catholic school led me to believe, he will do things when he's good and ready.

I will not wait for a man or anyone to make change happen. I am in control of this life, even in relationships with friends. I do not wait for them to make the friendship work. There are only so many times at bat with me before you strike out.

Zio Mike taught me that people, especially men, make time in life for the things they desire, whether it's a woman, friend, ballgame or beer. Everything is a matter of priorities and when someone cannot fit you into their life then they do not consider you a priority.

Maybe I believe that I deserve to be a priority because as the first grandchild of an Italian-American family, I was lovingly called their "Number One" or Princess by *Nonno*. The Number One part must have grated on the last nerve of my sister and cousins but let me tell you that each of us, individually, was treated as Number One.

As I travel this world, I now know what a rare gift my family was to me. Supporting and nurturing us with that kind of love is a priceless treasure. Not once growing up did I ever think I was second to anything in my parents' lives. Not once did I call either of them at work and be told that I would have to wait while they did something more important. No, the call was always taken by them so that they could hear my voice. Then, with an assurance that my life was not in danger, they would tell me they would call me back, if necessary.

My college boyfriend was like that. I was the only priority in his life, so much so that he would call me two, three, four times a day just to hear my voice...for seven years. As a young girl in my 20s, I didn't appreciate that and felt suffocated.

Sometimes the right person comes along at the wrong time. Sometimes the right person comes along and their development is not synchronistic with yours. Sometimes the right person comes along and realizes that change is necessary because there is never a right time and we must seize a precious moment and make it work.

We should not toil and struggle to force a relationship to jive. However, it takes effort to make something grow over time. Sadly, we are an instant soup society. In the U.S., we have boil-in-bag rice, microwaves and drive-thru windows for fast food. Here in Italy, life moves at a much slower pace. Heck, the rice comes raw and they don't even print directions on the box, so everything comes through trial and error. As a side note, the damn rice is causing a lot of error despite numerous trials!

"Spero e Sogno"

Love doesn't just happen,

we create it as we go.

We nurture and shape it day by day,

journey by journey.

It's ever-changing and forever growing.

Road-bumps add character.

Rest-stops add flourish.

Love hurts - it heals

Love cries - it smiles

Love is jealous - it is trusting

Love leaves you empty - it fulfills you.

Yet, you know you have it just right

when two hands can hold it at a distance and

feel each other's heart and soul across the sea.

Chapter 6 - Pasta, Piove e Molto Pacienza

am channeling my inner *Nonna*. Grandma and *Zia Anna* would both be proud of my well-honed cooking and laundry skills, learned lovingly at their knees.

This is the 21st century except in the south of Italy, where clothes dryers don't exist and you must hang out the wash. That becomes something of a challenge when the spring rains have not let up in three weeks. Nothing ever dries, inside or out. You begin to feel as though rheumatism will set in because everything feels cold and damp when you get dressed in the morning. What do they say? Cold bras, warm heart!

"Ah, you know, we open the window from the top when we dry the clothes in the house," my landlady lovingly explains.

"*Si, Si,*" I respond, "*ma piove fuori e piove dentro.*"

"*Lasciala stare*," let it be, I think to myself, rather than explain that even the air outside is too moist to help vent wet laundry inside.

My major accomplishment this week has been learning how to use the *lavatrice*, since the manual is in *tutto italiano*. Success! The clothes may be wet but they are clean.

My childhood was one full of love. It came at a time when *Nonna* and *Zia* watched and taught the kids after school, while Mom went to work. It was the best of Italian living amid a changing mindset for their newly adopted American home in the United States.

Here, I am truly returning to those roots since each night I must light the stovetop burners with a match to be able to cook. I remember being terrified each time *Nonna* had to light the stove's pilot light at the old country house. It never exploded and I learned more by watching her than I ever realized.

There is no such thing as canned soup in Italy and it was at least two weeks and a dozen trips to the *supermercato* before I realized that they at least sold bullion. In the meantime, I made *Nonna's zuppa di pollo* from scratch and Mom's masterful lentil soup. Only I think that I actually bested

Mom. You don't have to soak the lentils for an hour. Just start cooking.

Just like *Nonna*, I am again enjoying the art of cooking, even if it's only for me. While I may not be able to find things like canned kidney beans and cumin for a good chili on these cold, spring nights, I can easily find *fiori di zucchini*, in season, routinely, at the *supermercato*.

Sauté finely chopped onion; scramble two eggs; mix in some grated pecorino and chopped *fiori*; garnish with sea salt and pepper and I am in *frittata* heaven.

New York could not easily assimilate to a four hour lunch with a siesta. The world of high finance would come to a screeching halt, but I have quite easily acclimated to it, halting without screeching.

I am also enjoying my daily reunion with carbs - pasta, potatoes and rice. I am embracing every calorie of Italian cooking. Rocco had taught me his mother's recipe of boiled potatoes with lettuce and olives, tossed with olive oil and apple cider vinegar and whatever else was in the fridge. Now, I am addicted to this quickie, carb-enriched salad. Who needs croutons?

I had fully planned to bake while I was enjoying my new life, having brought pecans and walnuts with me because of the high price of nuts here. However, I can't figure out the baking powder and baking soda issue, nor can I successfully explain it to anyone. Note to self: *bring some Arm & Hammer the next time!*

The rain continues and so does the cooking. There is a reason that food and passion are so closely tied here. There is absolutely nothing else to do in bad weather except eat, make love and work, if you're lucky enough to have a man or a job. On second thought, some men are just plain work!

Believe it or not, despite the explosion of carbs, I am losing inches.

Carmine, the local *sarto*, shakes his head each time I pay him a visit with a new pair of *pantaloni* to alter.

"*Ma, non tu mangia?*" He asks with a smile.

"*Certo,*" as I shrug my shoulders, finding it hard to explain to him that I am losing all of this weight because I am walking at least five to six miles a day, not to mention visiting the gym three to four days per week. Although I firmly believe the caffeine and capsaicin cream, along with the Tummy Tuck Belt, jumpstarted this physio-thermic melting of my *corpo* before I ever left New York. Many laughed but I am a true believer now.

"*Tu sei bellissima.*"

Have I told you how much I adore this man?

"*Donne che non mangiano sono stupido.*"

"*Si, si,*'" I agree. He should only know how much I am eating, having found a new *pasticceria* on my way home from the gym. It's just not fair.

I have also learned not to ever, ever waste a trip climbing the hill to the villa when I pass the *supermercato*, each time I venture out. It is much easier to carry three or four things home than to try to do a week's worth of grocery shopping in one go, as I would at home. Besides, while I am quite talented at multi-tasking, I have yet to multi-juggle more than two bags of groceries and that damn, long skeleton key.

Recycling takes on new meaning here as well. In Sorrento, they have turned it into an art-form. There is *carta* (paper and cardboard), *umido organico* (organic food waste), *multi-materiale* (plastic and bottles) and *differenziata* for everything else. My favorite has to be the *umido*. Thank God, they pick that up twice a week or the house would stink.

I so want to pick up the rotting oranges and lemons which line my path each morning and night, like a mini obstacle course, as I toss out the *umido*. It seems like such a waste without squirrels, raccoons and rabbits to enjoy them.

Since they require all of this sorting and recycling, they pick up garbage seven nights a week, even in this down economy. It seems a bit ironic since the City of Naples has had issues with mounting garbage on the streets for the past several years. Here, however, it's all about the tourists and keeping the streets clean and safe for them, sorting the trash one bag at a time.

As the sun sets, the clouds come in and thunder rolls off the hills and so the ritual of the spring rains in Sorrento continues. It seems like it has rained for 40 days and nights, although it's been more like three weeks. The old stone and plaster walls of the villa do nothing but hold the dampness like a sponge. The calendar may say it is spring but winter has not released its sodden grip.

I feel as though I will never be warm again, inside or out. This gloom must yield to positivity and light soon. OK, now there is lightning, while thunder echoes off the mountains. It's enough to wake up that sleeping giant, *Vesuvio*, which sits across the bay. Note to self: *you must tackle that mountain while you're here!*

Oh, Lord, more lightning. I may have to shut down my lifeline for the night. My iPad and the Internet run twelve hours a day. They are my only connection to sanity right now.

My annual spring ritual to visit Rocco and the Amalfi Coast had not prepared me for the torrential rains which seem to have no let-up in sight. Each day I wake to grey clouds hanging low over the mountains. It's as if they cannot rise any higher and are trapped by a fortress of rock all around them.

By 10 o'clock each evening, the clouds, having long given up their fight to rise over the Lattaris, dump torrents of rain on Sorrento. It rains in sheets, vertically, horizontally, diagonally. I crawl under the covers counting the seconds between thunderbolts to see if the storm is moving away or getting closer.

"One-two-three...five-six-seven." I count in salsa time, hoping my passion in the dark will drown my anxiety.

I hear a trickle, *drip, drip, drip.* Where is it coming from? It sounds like drops of water are plopping onto the bed but the covers are dry. The ceiling above is apparently solid. *Drip, drip, drip. Da dov'è?* The villa may be 200 years old but this apartment was just newly renovated.

Drip, drip, swish! OK, now we are getting somewhere, as I hear the drips splash onto paper or something. I turn on the lights to investigate. There is a small puddle forming under my nightstand.

"*Ma, da dov'è?*"

There is no leak on the ceiling. There is no rivulet of water streaming down the wall.

Drip, drip, swish! I drop a towel onto the ice cold tile floor and hope to get through the night without being washed away.

The sun shines by late morning but it's deceiving because I can see the clouds, trapped against the rising mountains. There is no way out for them and by nightfall, they will display their wrath again. In the meantime, I make a break from this waterlogged fortress and ironically head for *il mare*. Somehow the sea always centers me and brings me peace.

Traces of a stormy night lie evident upon the shore. Peace washes in with the lap of each wave, as the tattered beams of a wooden ship are battered about, tied in seaweed and debris. Life moves on amid the rubble and all each of us can do is live each day to the fullest, aware of the brevity of its beauty.

If we can rise each day ready to inhale the energy and experiences we are presented with and go to bed each night knowing we have lived, loved and shared as honestly as possible, then we have done good...not only for ourselves but for each other. There is no lifeguard on duty. We each swim at our own risk during this short journey. It is our decision, alone, whether to swim against the tide.

Italians, even the young, are not so willing to change, to swim against the tide. It is the Italian culture to suffer rather than modify or evolve. They do not suffer in silence. They suffer together, on the streets, in the piazzas or at the *tabacchi*. These are the places you will hear lively, sometimes short, sometimes lengthy but always animated discussions, bemoaning the state of the economic "crisis," and boy, do they love to use that word.

They cry about the failing *Circumvesuviana* rail line and hold meaningless transportation strikes which yield nothing in the way of progress. They argue over last night's match for S.S.C. Napoli but will almost always agree that the triumvirate of Cavani-Hamsik-Lavezzi is the south's Holy Trinity to *calcio*, futbol, soccer or whatever it's called.

Italians see obstacles and stare at them. Americans see walls and knock the damn things down. Maybe the solution lies somewhere in the middle, which is why I am truly working toward greater patience this trip!

La Primavera

Springtime arrives on the Amalfi Coast with a wisp of the scent of orange blossoms mixed with wisteria. Its dreamlike perfume offers the promise of sunlight and warmth in this *paradiso*. Then the rains come, storming down off the mountains and blowing blossoms and scent away until the next torrent. The season is changing slowly and I am certainly ready for its uplifting first blush.

Spring, here, is my favorite time of year. There is so much promise and expectation of great things to come. The heady perfume of the tiny white blossoms stays with us until the summer's heat will dry their bloom. The romance of the day's floral essence gives way to the passion of the night. This is Italy. This is the south of Italy. If the landscape of human emotions were to exist in a country, it would be in Italy.

Italian is getting easier for me. "*Si, si*" and "*certo*" get me through most situations. As for the rest, I just go with the flow, knowing that Italians will always try to help you when they see you struggle with their language.

"*Grazie, Dio.*"

I have stopped feeling sorry for myself, missing the family holidays of my youth and the routine of seeing familiar faces. Instead I am embracing the new and I am beginning to fit in. Even the dog in the *piccola strada* outside my window just looks at me whenever I pass, rather than chasing and barking after me, as he often does with strangers. *Piano, piano*, everything in time.

I am capitalizing on the isolation to have conversations with myself. I am listening to my own voice again without the white noise of public opinion. Channeling this newfound freedom enables me to focus on writing again.

Work is so much a part of who we are that it often becomes the predominant part of our life because it is necessary for our survival. Yet, without work to focus on, we are free to explore our life's purpose. Work is the lifeline but it is not a life.

Writing, on the other hand, is not just what I do but it is who I am, as much as any musician or painter is an artist, so it is with writers. Musicians have notes. Painters have paint. Writers have words.

I have been drafting stories since I learned to write. My parents must have known from when I first popped out because for my third Christmas they gave me a typewriter and a tape deck. Not your typical toddler toys, eh?

Yet, I had forgotten the joy of writing. I had spent the better part of 15 years taking care of everyone but myself.

Life often gets in the way and blocks your true passion but no more. Not for me.

However, despite this freedom, I couldn't sleep last night. When I finally turned on the light, I realized why. Outside, it was still and silent, unusual after three weeks of rain. Then I realized how life is like the rain.

A good cry washes over the soul like the rain pouring down. When it's over, there is a newness about the moment and a light which shines in a different way. In that dawn, there is the peace of a new beginning.

Like the rain, we become used to the tempest in our lives. We adjust and begin to schedule our lives around it. The storm doesn't stop us; it just becomes the constant drone in our lives which serves to slow us down. When it stops, we are so shocked into how easy life becomes that we actually miss the fury and don't know how to manage without it. However, we need to breathe and inhale the moment to gather ourselves in the light of a new day so that we may accomplish what we need to before the next tempest comes…and it will come…it always does.

Chapter 7 - Dancing with My Heart

ove gives you wings, but it also binds you. It binds you to someone, making you vulnerable to that one person in ways that others do not get to see.

I am forever bound to this place for it is here where my story begins. Here where the azure sea meets the blue sky, my heart beats in time with the lapping of the waves. My life ebbs and flows and takes on the local rhythm. Nothing is pressing. Life is too short. Anything important can be summed up in the brevity of a sun-kissed afternoon or the tidal pull of each wave of passion.

My world is different because of Rocco. The curves of his lips are the roadmap to tomorrow. Each kiss breathes life into this tired heart. It is rescue. It is home.

This great romance is the stuff of novels; yet, this is my reality.

"One-two-three…five-six-seven."

It started with onboard salsa and now I fuel my passion at Pakitos's Club in Pompei. Who could have imagined that when a boy asked a girl to dance four years ago that she would be living in Italy, let alone taking salsa lessons in Pompei?

In New York, I have always struggled with learning the salsa rhythm On1 from ballroom professionals versus On2 from club teachers. Timing is easier On1 but turns are easier On2. Now, toss in Italy and they have women's timing starting back On2, on the left foot.

"But this is New York Style," Pakito lovingly teases me, as he tries to make me feel at ease with my missteps in a studio crowded with strangers.

"Not for this New Yorker."

"OK, it is Lisa On1 and 2," and the whole class laughs at this *straniera salsera*.

I hold my own on that first night of intermediate class. I am dancing to my own rhythm and very comfortable with the internal tempo.

This was Rocco's school but he was nowhere in sight. Pakito understood enough of my translated heartbreak woes to keep us separate. My relationship with Pakito started as just a travel client but he has become a good friend. I'll keep dancing as if no one is watching and just hope the right dance partner enters my life.

Salsa and dancing are so much a part of my passion in life that I need a man who shares that interest...and who is hopefully a good leader. We all need good leaders, don't we?

They always teased me in dance class because I would lead when I first started six years ago. Sometimes strong women need to just let the man be the man.

I am strong, fiercely independent and economically self-sufficient. It should leave most men wondering where they fit in; yet, the right man would fit just right without feeling threatened or emasculated. That is a strong man - confident in himself and loving of his woman, whatever their respective roles.

Women in Italy don't have strong role models so they don't know that they can be and do anything that they want to do. I remember *Signor Snuggles,* a cute Italian rebound guy. He and I were in bed one night and he was shocked that I had always lived in my apartment alone. He was so shocked that he asked me twice. I only needed to imagine once that he still lived with his parents!

Couples don't need to share all of each other's passions. Yet, with something as sensual and romantic as dancing, especially Latin dancing, I think it would be a rare man who wouldn't mind seeing his significant other in the arms of other men every weekend. Dancers understand the need to try out other partners but non-dancers could easily get jealous.

Ah, wait a minute! Doesn't my vision of the need and sensuality of salsa dancing sound the same as the Italian male attitude toward sex or maybe any man's attitude toward sex? Maybe I should start looking at sex through the eyes of an Italian man to process the distinction from the typical female perspective.

There is an evolution to a woman's view of relationships that we do not truly appreciate until we are out of crisis mode, which wastes most of our 20s and 30s. It may sound cliché but it truly happens over time.

Looking back to my 20s, it was all about the fairytale, the perfect boyfriend, the perfect fantasy wedding, the perfect two children. Perfection resonated loud and clear and if something wasn't perfect, it was frustrating and led to great moments of angst. That is a word so synonymous with 20-somethings, as rebellious is to teenagers. Yet, perfection doesn't exist.

We seek out perfect advice from the worst people imaginable, other 20-somethings. We hash and rehash, verbatim, phone conversations which become the soundtrack to our desperate existence. It is amazing that we manage to attend college with such nonsense occupying most of our grey matter.

Our 30s are spent chasing things. Chasing a news story, chasing men, chasing success, chasing the baby clock, chasing the all-night dance caravan. The chase becomes so tiring and so time-consuming that we forget to focus on our life goals because we are chasing too many things in too many directions. If 30-somethings paused just long enough to breathe and focus, maybe the chase would not be so pressing and the goals would become clear.

Our 30s are occupied chasing men who are chasing their careers. There is nothing synchronistic about the relationship dance. We push and they run. We listen to that silent clock which we are led to believe ticks inside each of us. Yet, men hear that ultrasonic boom and run in the opposite direction. They withdraw prematurely and that's never a good thing in any situation. It works much the same way as those devices inserted into auto grills to repel deer. The Pest Repeller personified!

The worst part of the 30-something woman is that she then turns to other single, baby-crazed women and gay friends for advice. Wait, what?

We all have them, the gay boyfriend we turn to for gossip and fashion advice. I remember sitting in the Upper West Side apartment of my gay hairdresser in a panic as to why the hot, A-list rock star of the moment was not answering my twenty voice messages. When I then resorted to Plan B in a desperate effort to make this happen, I called Mom who knocked some sense into my head.

"Are you crazy? You don't ask a gay man for advice on how to get the attention of a straight man."

I laughed out loud, amid my nervous tears, then I quickly kissed my hairdresser goodbye and so went the 30s.

By our 40s, the chase has us running in circles to no avail. As for me, I was certain that a stint in law school would provide a solid foundation for the future. Note to self: *the next time you want to invest $75,000 in something, buy a diamond.*

The mental gymnastics of that venture were probably useful in helping me exercise my brain to ward off Alzheimer's, but who knew that a recession would hit New York lawyers and have me in need of a career infusion by the time my 50s rolled around? As to seeking advice, who had time with a full-time broadcasting job and law school?

Io ero pazza.

So, after having cared for the world and investing time and money in losing propositions, both in relationships and careers, I decided to focus on and fuel my passion for travel, which led me to Italy. It also provided an open door to expression, both written and verbal.

Exposing yourself to the world is not an easy exercise. The eagerness to write blends with reluctance to placing yourself in harm's way. You need to balance sharing yourself while maintaining your privacy.

As women, we often rely on and hide behind the men in our lives. Many of my contemporaries marvel at the independent streak which leads me to travel the world without seeking permission or financial support from anyone. When men want something, they buy it. When women want something, they ask for permission, whether it's from a parent, girlfriend or husband.

Stop thinking and asking and just start dancing.

"One-two-three...five-six-seven."

This is me and if I want your opinion, damn it, I'll give it to you!

Chapter 8 - It Happened by Chance

It happened by chance, just as it had started four years earlier. I had spent the past three-and-a-half weeks walking the streets of Sorrento hoping to see Rocco on every corner and there he was, standing onboard at the dock, as I went to board the ferry to *Ischia*.

I would know this man from across a football pitch, yet his New York Yankees cap flashed like a neon sign, as I closed in on Dock 4. The Yankees mean nothing to a man who grew up a world away but that cap means everything to him and it warmed my heart to see him wearing the gift I had given him three years earlier.

I didn't rush up the plank. Instead, I stood there, just gazing up at him, enjoying my first glimpse of him in a very long eleven months. I wanted to savor this moment because I knew things had changed between us and I didn't know how he would react. I didn't know if we could reconcile and I wanted to hold onto this point in time before our eyes found each other and before I knew whether our hearts could do the same.

The crowd anxiously awaited a ride to Capri, since this was the first bit of sunshine in nearly a month. I, on the other hand, was waiting for my Rocco, oh, and my ride to Ischia. I had seen the ferry earlier, as I descended the long walk down Via Marina Piccola, hoping that it was Rocco's boat, and my prayers were answered.

As the feisty mob boarded, I waited at the bottom of the plank and sure enough, Rocco began to hurry down. He is always rushing, always in a hurry. So much nervous energy stirs inside of him. He was rushing so fast that he ran right into me and was startled into reality with one look in my direction. His face went from concentrated stress to the huge smile which radiates from him to illuminate my core.

The change in our relationship was palpable. I went to grab him and not let go and although he hugged back, he gave me one of those Italian kisses on two cheeks, bestowed on everyone, including people they don't like.

"Ah, Lisa, you need a ticket? Wait, I'll be right back." He spit it out and was off like a jackrabbit. He was so fast that he didn't hear me say that I had already purchased one.

By the time he returned, his ship was ready to leave for Capri and I was left waiting on the dock for the boat to

Ischia with his promise that he would text me later. He did. That is one thing which is so atypical for most men. I might not always like what he has to say, but if Rocco says that he is going to do something, he always does it.

I spent an enjoyable day with friends for lunch and a spa escape at *L'Albergo Regina Isabella*, the site of our extremely romantic "mini-moon" last spring. I am glad that I had them to distract me and my anticipation of the rendezvous which I hoped would come later that evening.

The text came. His ship changed course and he was coming to get me. *Yeah*!

The stormy seas were the perfect stage for our reunion, bumpy for us and queasy for him. He has worked his entire adult life on ferries but still suffers from sea-sickness when the weather gets stormy. Yet, he could not do enough for me, offering me coffee and introducing me to the crew.

In the fifty-minute, stomach-churning ride back to Sorrento, he managed to catch me up on his life. He's working a second job to become a *pizzaiola* (although I already think he's the best chef in the world!) and he has been studying English twice a week…wait for it…with Catholic, American missionaries in Castellammare di Stabia. Missionaries? God does indeed answer prayers and works in mysterious ways.

This would be a long, tiring night for him, so he offered to take me to dance class in Pompei tomorrow. I took the train to Castellammare and he was there waiting for me on the platform even though I was a half-hour late. He did not sit in the car and wait. He met me on the platform in the damp, night air because he was worried about me at the unsafe station.

His dancing is so much better than mine, although we've both been dancing for six years. Latin dance is taken seriously here because it's one of the few forms of entertainment and there are so many clubs which offer it. His timing begins *a la sinistra* and front and mine is *a la destra* and back. I just hope we can get back on the same timing together.

One-two-three...five-six-seven.

Chapter 9 - Come Va

*G*etting around the ancient streets of southern Italy can be a challenge, with or without a car. Since driving a stick-shift still poses a test for this *straniera* and renting an automatic car is a luxury, I opted to truly live outside my comfort zone and use local transportation, with comfort being the operative word.

Trains

I know that I am supposed to be working on that virtue of patience but riding the *Circumvesuviana* can get on anyone's last nerve. The train line is right out of the 1960s and probably has not been updated since.

The *Circumvesuviana* is so-called because the line circumnavigates that sleeping giant of a volcano, *Vesuvio*, which looms around every bend. The line connects Sorrento with Naples, as well as other outlying areas of Napoli. The problem is that strikes are called with great frequency.

Workers who have a job strike because they are dissatisfied with conditions, while those who don't have a job often stage blockades on the tracks. The good thing is that in true Italian style, they announce the strike days before and the exact timing usually coincides with their need for *una siesta mezzogiorno*.

The challenge is that you can take the train in the morning and there may be no train to get you back home. Ah, the joys of life in Italy. *Pacienza, Lisa, molto pacienza.*

Packed like *alici* into a 40-to-50-year-old train, we tinker along to ancient Pompei. As we pass graffiti-sprayed stations like *Castellammare di Stabia, Meta and Torre Annunziata*, I wonder, if these ugly emblems of the ghetto will be discovered as the frescoes of the 21st century when they are unearthed in 2,000 years. Somehow, I expect they will endure because modern man cannot figure a way to eradicate this so-called street art.

The train here is great for people watching. It is a microcosm of life in Italy. There are tourists with the look of lost sheep and the smell of sunscreen, unheard of in Italy. There are panhandling gypsies with the look of desperation and the smell of body odor and cheap cologne. There are also teenagers with no look, the same all over the world.

Then there is the morning's entertainment. How can you possibly be in a bad mood for the day when accordion-playing gypsies start a rounding rendition of *"Funiculi Funicula?"* The real fun begins when teens, en route to school, hop onboard at *Piano di Sorrento* and begin singing *"Papa Americano."* It puts an instant smile on everyone's face, even the hardened Napoletani, who tire of this *divertiti* easily. I was actually sorry to see this hormone-fueled group exit the train halfway through my journey.

The stations reflect the neighborhoods. Sorrento is clean and all about the tourists but as we veer away from the peninsula, we enter the darkened tunnel. Just as we exit, beyond Castellammare, life comes in the form of graffiti and despair. Laundry hangs next to satellite dishes and I wonder if it ever gets clean with all of the soot stirred by the train. There are horses alongside the station at *Ponte Persica* and garbage tossed nearly everywhere en route to Napoli.

Headstrong Italians are very much stuck in the past but living in the moment. Come to think of it, that is exactly how I felt when I arrived here.

Why do they make life harder than it needs to be? Why do they insist on moaning rather than changing? This is where Italians differ greatly from Italian-Americans. My family recognized the hardships they faced in the south of

67

Italy and Sicily and chose to change their stars, so to speak. They packed everything they could into *una valigia* and shipped out in steerage. They boldly ventured into a new world, unsure of what they would find but with the certainty that anything would be better than life in Italy.

Only you can change your stars. Only you know what makes you happy inside. There is not one other person who can give you that gift. You need to sit alone in time and space and the answer comes in the solitude of your soul, in the complete isolation of your thoughts. That is where the seed is planted and the idea takes root.

I have been extremely lonely here at times, not one person in my own family even called for my birthday. Even Rocco, so wrapped up in his own *ansia*, forgot. The point is that we can only rely on ourselves. If someone is there to share and support our dream then that is a true gift from God. In the meantime, give unto yourself first and the rest will find its way.

Napoli

Did you ever meet someone and instantly know that if distance was not an issue that you would be best friends? Marina is that kind of person, at once warm and caring. She is a tour guide I had known online for several years but never met until I ventured to the dark side - Naples!

I had been to Naples before with Rocco and both he and *Signor Snuggles* warned me about venturing there alone, saying it was too dangerous. To be honest, my New York reporter chops don't scare easily but when the person you love most in the world suggests that it is not a safe place to visit, you tend to listen to them.

There is an old Italian saying: *"Vedi Napoli e poi muori"* ("See Naples and die"). Well, I figure proverbs are rooted in reality, over time. And since I remembered fondly my first visit to see an S.S.C. Napoli game at San Paolo Stadium, I thought the proverb should be changed to "*Go to the stadium in Naples and you may die!*" Surely, she gests, you think to yourself, but alas, there is that iota of truth in any proverb.

There was so much testosterone-fueled energy among the Napoli Ultras at that game that I thought I would die without the protective arms of Rocco to envelop me each time they neared a goal. I survived, but those images filled my mind as I boarded the train in Sorrento to venture into the bowels of Naples, solo for the first time. Remembering that soccer match, I imagined that the entire city was filled with drug-fueled, hormonal hoards of mad men roaming the streets.

Life is an adventure and I decided that the New Yorker in me, having survived shootouts in the South Bronx and the chase for escaped convicts from Sing Sing, could handle anything that she came upon in Naples. I nearly laughed when I alighted the train at Garibaldi Station and stood amid a busy, metropolitan, modern train depot with *polizia* at every 25 meters. This is the Naples they warned me about? You have got to be kidding!

I had to memorialize this with a camera and sure enough, with the first glimpse of "tourist" in the air, three gypsies came out of nowhere, panhandling me for money. They were from eastern Europe, however, and not Italian, and once I dismissed them in raging Italian, they went their merry way. The Sicilian curse words I learned as a kid now come in handy!

Marina introduced me to a different side of this city. She showed me her city and what a city is Naples. Its global reputation as a dark and dangerous city must be based on years past. True, the garbage problem still exists but each major city has its own albatross and for Naples it's the *camorra* and garbage. Why is the mob always associated with hauling trash? Definite fodder for another tale.

As a seasoned New Yorker, the only real challenge for me was navigating Naples' timeworn streets. The ancients did not number them for 21st century visitors and, as in most of Italy, the streets bear the names of a local church, piazza or historic event which occurred on the spot.

Marina's knowledge is priceless. She knows every inch of her hometown from when the Greeks and Egyptians occupied it, to where there is a hidden Caravaggio painting, and the location of the most recently uncovered, underground *scavi*.

We visited *presepe* alley, Via San Gregorio Armeno, where nativity sets are born; Via Duomo, the matrimonial highway of bridal salons; and *L'Ospedale delle Bambole*, a 150-year-old-doll hospital. Had I known about this hidden treasure, *Nonna's* doll would have accompanied me on this trip because she is in serious need of a facelift after fifty years. Yeah, aren't we all?

I found Naples to be a fascinating, typically Italian city where modern clashes with antiquity and where cars clash with pedestrians on its narrow streets.

"Guarda, guarda," I scream as the passing car's mirror slams into my shoulder with a whack hard enough to tip me over.

"*Signora, scusa, scusa.*" The two *strunzi* stop but I give them the Sicilian death stare and they know enough to run, lest I change my mind and call the *polizia*. There were enough witnesses on the busy, but very narrow, Via dei Tribunali.

Marina urges me to sue, "You're a lawyer; you know what to do."

"Yes, I do and sometimes, you know when to walk away."

My day ends the way it started, onboard a crowded train. The system is so tenuous that schedules don't matter because the train in one direction will not depart the station until a train from the opposite direction materializes, lest there be no trains at all.

I always feel like I need a shower in this roving box of sinew and stink. I yearn to shake off the ride immediately and lo and behold, if it's an April evening, the rains come. I was drenched before making my climb up to the villa. God really does have a strange sense of humor.

Will I return to Naples? By train, this train? I don't know. What I do know is that city dwellers the world over seem to like staying put. My friends who live in Manhattan always think suburbanites need to take a train into town to see them but always make excuses when invited to "the country." It is the same in Naples. They say they can't take the whole day to come to the coast but clearly think it's OK for me to spend ninety minutes on this country's poor train system to trek to see them. *Come va?*

Buses

Hopping on a bus in Italy is also quite an experience since most of the drivers pretend to know nothing more than their own route, so asking for directions is a waste of time. Individual bus strikes can also take place even in busy Rome, where my driver decided one night that he had enough. Picture it - Thursday evening rush hour in busy Rome, I board a bus crammed with tired Romans at the end of a long work day. The driver pulls over to the next *firmata*; parks the bus; and gets out.

Ten of us wait and wait. The locals are too tired to raise a ruckus and this *straniera* is too ignorant to realize this driver is not coming back. We are way too far from the historic center for me to hike back and forget about trusting any Roman taxi driver to take me on a wild goose chase as the meter ticks away. So, we wait and wait some more.

A half-hour goes by before an old man boards the bus. Not a driver, not a bus official, just a little old man.

'*Sera, è necessario andremo su quella bus di fronte.*

Like mesmerized children following the piper, not a word is spoken. We all get up and board the bus parked in front. The doors close and off we go, none of us realizing that this is not the right bus and we are then dropped off on the opposite side of the city. *Mamma mia!* Roman adventures happen here when you least expect them.

I also eventually learned to heed the warning of the bus Nazis in the Eternal City. These undercover monitors patrol the bus system, nabbing unsuspecting tourists and sneaky locals who buy one ticket or no ticket and then ride around the city all day for free. Generally, with tourists, they let you slide and only ask you to pay the fare right there on the spot.

Napoletani, on the other hand, have a different code. They don't even buy the ticket and confidently get on and off the bus like it's a free shuttle. This day I disembarked from the ferry on Ischia and immediately bought my €1.30 ticket at the *biglietteria*. So, why didn't I punch it when I boarded the bus? Who knows? Living like a local now, I am in that Napoletani mindset. I held the ticket in my hand and as these two *Ischitani* pricks boarded the bus, they demanded my documents. What the hell? Seriously?

They saw the ticket in my hand and approached me with this sneering look in their eye. They were dressed like tourists and displayed no authoritative badge, yet every local on the bus knew that they were the bus Nazis.

I explained in fervent English that I forgot to punch it in the machine.

"*Documenti*," they insisted.

Really, are you kidding me? I am holding a beach bag with a towel sticking out of it. Do they think I'm carrying "*documenti*" with my flip-flops?

"*Documenti mia in l'albergo*," I say and again they just look at me.

"*Dov'è?*"

"*Sorrento.*"

They obviously did not like that answer and continue leering at me. Do those stupid leers really intimidate anyone? I wanted to laugh, despite my annoyance at their arrogance. My New York wanted to get all up in their face but I thought better of it.

The more I explained in two languages, the angrier these idiots became. A local woman, who did not speak any English, even tried to reason with them on my behalf but they became more and more agitated. I said I had no money to pay the damn €37.80 fine and their quick reply was that there was a *Bancomat* at the *porto*. Well, now, how convenient! And where did they come up with that odd figure for a penalty? I figure the amount of the fine was what one or both of them needed to take the *moglie* out for a Friday night pizza and this *straniera* would pay for it. One thing being a lawyer teaches you, contrary to what the public-at-large believes, there are some battles just not worth fighting.

Sita buses are another trip, literally and figuratively. These local buses enable you to travel between the Sorrentine Peninsula and further down the Amalfi Coast without having to take a ferry. During the off-season, the boats don't even run between Sorrento and Positano and Amalfi so using *Sita* is the only way to get around.

The schedule isn't too bad but these routes are often crowded with tourists. The crammed buses will fly right by a stop, leaving locals who need to get to work or appointments stranded for the next thirty minutes. The tourists onboard think it's quite humorous and wave to the poor souls who will hopefully be able to board the next bus.

In places like Positano, it's knowing where to wait that can make the difference between boarding a return bus home or waiting again! It's worth it to climb the hill and board the bus at *Sponda* because you're more likely to get on than if you wait for the bus to retrieve you at the *Chiesa* stop.

I don't really miss driving. Walking has paid off in all of the inches I have lost along the way. Every single pair of size six jeans has been taken in by Carmine, so why do I now have a *ponza* that wasn't there when I arrived? The hips have slimmed to a four and the *ponza* has, well, it has *ponza-ed*. It is so not fair.

Here, all of the men will tell you to eat because you are on vacation. Rocco's theory is to eat now because then you get old and die and can't eat anymore. Meanwhile, they are not salivating over the larger women. They drool over the skinny girls, go figure.

I enjoy the exercise but it would be nice to get behind the wheel of a sports car, even with gas at about $10.00 a gallon.

I come alive when I drive these ancient roads and *La Costiera Amalfitana*. Many friends back home think I'm crazy and wonder how I could possibly enjoy driving on streets meant for horse carts with drivers meant for the loony bin! Even the locals avoid driving *La Costiera Amalfitana*, when possible.

OK, do they know me? I'm a NYC street reporter. We drive commando and make Napoletani look tame, even here in *che è pazzo* land.

When I drive down from Rome, each and every time, the knot starts to leave the back of my neck as I come upon the Apennine Mountains, along the A3 toward Napoli, but my soul doesn't find peace until I hit *La Costiera Amalfitana*.

Now, I know that road like the back of my hand and I never tire of its twists and turns; its death-defying cliffs; and its complete blackness in the dead of night. It's as mysterious as the people who inhabit its villages, like *Praiano, Minori, Maiori* and *Furore*, not to mention tourist-trodden Amalfi and Positano.

Here, the people are passionate; the love is wild; and the scenery leaves you breathless. The locals either welcome you immediately or forever gaze at you from a distance, even if they have known you for years.

La Costiera Amalfitana, The Amalfi Drive, reflects the soul of its people. Its spirit echoes in the cliffs, which rise toward *Ravello*, or sinks toward the Bay of Naples. You are at once master of its complexities or forever fearful of its surprises…and for those who fail to see it for sitting on the floor of a tour bus, I wish you could see it through my eyes.

Capri

Capri, for me, is where God came down and kissed my soul one spring day. It is where I came alive again. This is where time stopped as an Italian boy asked an American girl to dance onboard as if no one was watching. This morning, four years later, he took my hand again to help me board the ferry to return.

This island of the rich and famous oozes romance and relaxation. I do not need to visit its sites or shop in the quaint hillside town of *Anacapri*. For me, I ride the *Funicolare* up and my stress goes down. The closer to Via Tragara that I get, the more I inhale the perfume that is Capri.

Each part of the Amalfi Coast has its own scent. In Sorrento, it is orange and lemon blossoms. On Ischia, it is jasmine. Here on Capri, it is wisteria and although I have returned late in its season, the light essence of its periwinkle blooms still hangs in the air.

Wisteria

Under a canopy of dangling wisteria,

gentle waves echo the beat of your heart.

This heady aroma blankets me in euphoria,

for it's perfection this place imparts.

And you - you made me fall in love with you.

Now, it is only you I see, between these petals.

Only you amid the purple and the blue,

Only you and at once this bliss settles me.

Via Tragara gives way to Via Faraglioni. The cliff walk winds its way around the rugged coast until the massive stones come into view. *Gabbiani* cry, as they fly around the trio of giant rocks they call home, while tiny motor boats and tourist ferries circle them from the sea.

I was renewed. I was energized. I would descend 300 meters just to take photos from the beach. Wait, what? *Sono pazza*? If I descend, I must later ascend, on foot, no donkeys, no boyfriend as a crutch! I would do this on my own.

The path winds its way down the cliff. Each level gives pause, as the turquoise waters flow closer and closer and the sound of the waves crashes on the shore. If bliss could be a color, today would be Amalfi blue.

Ristorante Da Luigi comes into view and I think this physical activity will surely be rewarded with a very expensive *caffè freddo*. *Allora*, Luigi is still in springtime hibernation and I press on, now less than thirty meters from the water.

It's just me and a fisherman at sea level. He's alone with his fish and I'm alone with the sea, and Francie, Barbie's cousin. She has become my travel companion in the last few years. I take her everywhere. She travels light, always wears the same turquoise-colored, Amalfi blue outfit, *apro-*

pos, and she never complains. I am now in the habit of photographing her at every iconic world site. Most people shake their head that a grown woman carries and photographs a doll on her travels. As for Rocco, he just smiles.

The sea is wonderfully calming, as it thrashes about with no rhyme or reason. If you allow yourself to fall into its rhythm, it hypnotizes you, erasing all thoughts except the rapture of its power, that raw power. It's reaffirming and awakens in me the energy to climb again, 300 meters, up the rugged terrain.

I stop along the way. The way up is always tougher than the way down, for anything. *Penso di si.* We struggle to make it, to advance to that next rung on the ladder of success. Then, when we reach our destination, it never seems to be enough. We always want more, not realizing that sometimes we are, already, just where we should be.

Via Tragara is again in view and I can stop climbing, stop trying to capture this day in photos and just etch the memory in my heart. This place, that man, they are in my soul forever, no matter the outcome of this journey.

Roma

There is a convenience to living anywhere in Europe. Within a short amount of time you can travel to a new country and experience the tastes, sensations and customs of a different culture. With that benefit in mind, I decided to explore Rome and get my taste of city life again, away from the coast, which sometimes seems like another country in Italy.

I decided the bus from Sorrento was the most economical and direct way to get to the Eternal City, even if it takes an eternity to get there.

I set out in the morning darkness and took a left turn into hell. At 5:00 am, a small crowd gathered outside the Sorrento *stazione*. The damp air heightened the dank stench of body odor mixed with cheap cologne, which hung inside the bus like the fetor of death inside a morgue.

These giants of the trail ways are not meant to navigate the narrow side-streets of the Sorrentine Peninsula. We swayed, back and forth, to and fro, until I thought I would lose my hurried breakfast of a stale croissant and black coffee. My God, just listen to that, I am becoming Italian, bite by bite.

The cacophony of pre-dawn cell phone chatter assaulted my being. Even the octogenarian *nonna*, who boarded with her frail husband, *piano, piano*, was handling calls with the agility of a Park Avenue madame. Who could she possibly be speaking with, and so often, at 5 am?

The 20-something girls next to me surrounded me with their senseless babble. *Chiacchieroni.* People often talk just to have something to do but it's 5 o'clock, why don't they just sleep on the bus? Cranky was an understatement and before we stopped midway at the Autogrill, I had lost that unpalatable breakfast into the baggie which had carried it only ninety minutes earlier.

"Oh, God, are we there yet?"

Hours seemed like an eternity but as soon as I dropped anchor at my hotel and washed the ride from my spirit, I was off and running. The New Yorker in me was pulsing again, the energy of this fantastic city flowing through my veins, camera in hand.

Rome is an eternal photo op. There is history and mystery at each corner. There is a labyrinth of wonder which lies just a meter or so below your feet, if you just watch where you are walking, literally.

I thought the day would be just another rainy day of shopping along Via del Corso, amid throngs of annoying tourists. At first, I stepped inside the cloister of the *Doria Pamphilj Gallery* just to get out of the rain. True, it houses one of the largest art collections in the city and spans four centuries, but I just wasn't into art this day. I truly just sought shelter in the rain.

84

I re-grouped and it wasn't until I rejoined the wet mass of humanity on the Corso that I came upon the church of wonder next door, *Santa Maria in Via Lata*.

I spied a lone man sitting in the external entry at a table. He was bored and the sign in Italian indicated there was something to see downstairs for just a few euros. As a photo-journalist, I learned a long time ago to always look up and down, and backwards, when standing in a new spot. That is often where the most interesting subjects are discovered.

Feeling like Indiana Jones' kid sister, I descended down the ancient, stone steps. I could feel this was something special and had no idea just how special until I stepped back 2,000 years into the time of the Apostles. I was awestruck. This was where Saint Luke wrote his tales for the Bible. This was where he hosted Saint Peter and where it is believed that Saint Paul was under house arrest for two years. They even discovered the chain they suspect was used by a Roman soldier for that purpose...no electronic ankle bracelets in those days.

The altar is still *in situ* and fonts for holy water are still attached to the wall, as they were in biblical Rome. This is fascinating for a Catholic school survivor. Every kid has a favorite saint and Saint Paul was mine because he was a romantic. Sure, he preached ancient church dogma; heck, he created it, all of that nonsense about a woman cleaving unto a man and hence she belongs to him…whatever, he made you think:

> "13:8 Love never fails. But where there are prophecies, they will be done away with. Where there are various languages, they will cease. Where there is knowledge, it will be done away with. 13:9 For we know in part, and we prophesy in part; 13:10 but when that which is complete has come, then that which is partial will be done away with."
>
> - First Corinthians

He preached these words to whomever sought counsel here, in ancient Rome, just a meter or so below where mere mortals walk today.

The rainy day led into the mist-soaked night, which beckoned me to stroll the streets of Rome with camera at the ready. I started my evening *passeggiata* on the west side of the Ponte Pallatino. The Tiber River looks especially lovely under the cloak of darkness. Somehow the moonlight disguises the muck, which the sunlight seems to bring into focus.

I turned left upon reaching Via Luigi Petroselli, after stopping to admire the second century *Temple of Portunus*, which honored the god of the ancient port nearby. I reflected how 2,000 years has changed this very spot from a port marketplace to one of the busiest thoroughfares in central Rome. Walking Via Luigi Petroselli is perfectly safe. Trying to cross it in between racing *motos* is another story.

I stroll on toward *Teatro Marcello*, lovely and glistening in the evening light. It's an open air theater built in 13 B.C. which now houses luxury apartments. What would Caesar think of condos? It resembles the Colosseum and Romans love making fun of tourists who think it is. Ask any taxi driver and he'll tell you with a smirk on his face, "S*i, si, it is the mini Colosseo!"* Make no mind; the natives make fun of tourists all over the world.

Sempre dritto, straight on, umbrella in hand, I seem to be losing my battle to stay dry. The rain pours down but does not dampen the romance of this evening. Romance is where you find it, even if you are alone. Those who disbelieve such notions are not visionaries. The pure definition of romance is the colorful narrative created of an imagined world. If you do not allow yourself to dream, especially in color, then you cannot possibly understand.

I walk on and imagine myself surrounded by toga-wearing men and women, speaking an ancient Latin dialect.

Do their dreams differ that much from mine? Did ancient men and women have as much trouble as we do today?

Others question how I can possibly find romance anywhere without someone beside me. Clearly, their happiness is tied up outside of their being, whereas mine is in my soul.

I pass the busy Piazza Venezia and look up to see the lit Monument to Vittorio Emanuele. I marvel at the monument's ceiling frescoes which I had never noticed before in the daylight. Stop, look, listen because there is so much to perceive in a new light, even at night.

After passing the backside of the *Foro Romano*, where food trucks and umbrella hawkers are about the only souls out tonight, the Colosseum lies straight ahead of me in all its majesty. It still takes my breath away, especially at night. This night in particular, as the rain poured down, there was nary a tourist anywhere. It was strange to have the entire plaza to myself and I still didn't think twice about being a single woman in Rome at night.

I feel safe here, away from judgmental eyes, alone to create my new world. Tonight, my visions are through the viewfinder. Shadows and raindrops cast the monuments and ancient side-streets in a different light. It's not an ominous light but a mysterious one, full of secrets and clandestine affairs.

Soaking now and feeling very much in need of a hot pot of tea, I start to head back. The camera tucked safely away, I am left in my thoughts. Down past *Arco di Costantino*, I hug the outer wall of the Forum on Via di San Gregorio. My mind plays tricks on me. I conjure up ghosts of Roman senators and patricians whose spirits are still so evident here, still so alive, as if to beckon me to enter the gated excavation and uncover a mystery.

Swoosh, splat! A passing taxi splashes me back to reality, and again, I find have come full circle tonight.

London

From Rome, I hopped a plane to London and was immediately at home again. When I planned this spring fling into the unknown, I had actually thought London would be a good midterm break and I could not have been more right.

The homesickness I had been feeling on the Amalfi Coast disappeared in London, where I am at once at ease. English television, American shows without overdubbing and a proper bubble bath offer sheer bliss!

London was where my first soul-searching venture toward independence had taken me at the ripe age of 21. Here is where I now go for mental and emotional support when feeling lonely and out of my comfort zone.

Returning to my familiar neighborhood of Bloomsbury and Gordon Square, I enjoy the walks through the park where Virginia Woolf, Oscar Wilde and Charles Dickens used to roam. Their presence is still so much a part of this corner of literary London and maybe that's why I feel so at home here. My imagination lets go and I am free to relax to wherever it takes me.

As a student, I would imagine the conversations enjoyed by the Bloomsbury Group over a cuppa at the Hotel Russell, discussing the politics and mores of the day or other-worldly musings enjoyed by spiritual Victorians. During one outing I happened upon what would become my secret corner of London, the place to head for solitude when escaping the student blues of study abroad.

The old *Church of Christ the King* holds reign at a corner of Gordon Square, not far from my first student apartment. It's constructed of the lovely ocher-colored Bath stone, which makes it warm and inviting despite its massive size.

In the past, I was enchanted by its gabled spires and corner turrets. I entered its open door and found the most lovely chapel to sit and contemplate life, as only a 20-year-old can do, full of angst and awe. The chapel's walls were lined with little seating nooks to hold only one person, as if enveloping them in their thoughts and sheltering them from the outside world.

Today, I returned home for my spiritual pilgrimage, happy to find another young student meditating in her nook, focusing on her life, as I had done so many years earlier. We each try to grab our piece of solitude to center our life in this crazy world.

Going home again is always good for the soul, walking in the footsteps of where I had ventured to London as a young student thirty years ago made me realize how far I have journeyed in this life. Then, I was an anxious 20-something, wondering when will I marry; who will I marry; how will I fit in; and thinking how much I missed home. Now, I am wondering if I even want to return home. My life is where I live. My family is my Mom and I take her with me everywhere, thanks to VOIP, voice over Internet protocol. I am responsible for my own happiness and as far as I have traveled, I still have many more miles to go and places to see.

Sure, I would now like to share this journey with someone and my heart is sad when I go to speak and the room is silent, but that will not keep me from making noise. Your heart still beats even with severed cords. It might not sing as easily but it flutters and brings you joy and when you smile from within good things come to you from without. Just breathe, your music will come.

Chapter 10 – 'Torno a Sorrento

returned to Sorrento with new resolve, this time sitting at the front of the bus. That's what I will do from now on; always aim for the front of the bus. Life is too short to lag in the rear, guessing what might be around the next bend in the road.

London awakened my focus. I had to make the most of the next month because time would lapse all too quickly.

I returned to the villa on Sunday evening, the warm weather brought more people out and about. This is the south of Italy and Sunday is still all about families. Yet, too many families are struggling in this economy, trying to make sense out of years of working and contributing to a corrupt political machine.

As in the United States, many Italians are going to sleep hungry and many others are choosing to end their lives, as the suicide rate rises in proportion to the unemployment rate. In the United States there's an unwritten media code and we don't broadcast suicides. In Italy, they headline the news almost every night during these difficult times.

There is a conflicted spirit about this place. There is the ever-present worry and reluctance to change anything; therefore, what you are left with is a society deeply anchored to the past and trying to cope with the present.

Tonight, as the sun sets over Sorrento, I stroll Via degli Aranci for an evening *passeggiata*. I hear the faint melody of "*'Torno a Surriento*" from an accordion in the distance and relish how this Napoletani tableau comes to life before my eyes.

As I walk further from the villa, the melodic strains come closer. The golden hue of sunset in Sorrento warms the street as the scene brightens my heart. It is my favorite time of day here. On the corner a man is playing for his supper. Outside an apartment building, he stands, playing, smiling, and hoping that someone will help him tonight. A family of three generations watches in appreciation from their balcony and when the music stops, a basket of food is lowered in generous acknowledgment. This scene would play out much differently in New York and tonight I am content to be here.

I find myself in front of the cinema I had passed often during my rainy day walks. This is the center of Sunday society. In a small city with nothing else to do, going to the movies is an event whether you are eight or 80, single or coupled.

My everyday Italian has improved enough so that I can now explain my needs to a shopkeeper and they understand and offer assistance. That is why tonight I thought I would venture out with new resolve and tackle a movie in Italy, where everything is over-dubbed and there are no subtitles.

This is unlike your megalithic American cinema. This is a decent sized theater in the heart of Sorrento which probably has not been refurbished since the 1970s. There is no tiered seating and the seats don't have cup-holders because there is no concession stand. People are actually here to watch a movie.

"Yeah, no annoying popcorn eaters," she says, hopefully, and at only €7, it's a risk worth taking.

It's the first night of Woody Allen's new flick, "To Rome with Love." *Perfetto*, don't you think?

This is a film for all ages…at least in Sorrento. It is an event! The lights dim and the glow of cell phones reminds me that I can still be irritated while watching a movie. As the opening credits begin to roll, the audience sings along with the opening bars to "*Volare.*"

"*Volare, whoa, oh, cantare, oh, oh, oh, oh. De blu, de pinto de blu...*"

It's so cool. Everyone is singing and I have a lump in my throat. I smile in the dark theater and suddenly feel like I belong here - they're all nuts. Same picnic, just a different blanket...and with better food!

It has only taken me six weeks but Sorrento is starting to feel like home now.

"*Ciao,*" I wave to the security guard who mans the booth at an apartment building on Viale Montariello.

"'*Giorno,*" he smiles back. The morning ritual now happens two to three times a day, as I climb up and down this hill of mine. Climbing up and down, rolling with the flow, living very much in the moment without a plan. Each day presents new challenges and new experiences. It is how we choose to manage these events which either turns them into stepping stones or roadblocks.

I had not heard from Rocco in two weeks so I decided I would venture to the port for a ferry to Ischia. I would just buy a one-way ticket in case he was there, minimizing my loss on all fronts, so to speak!

Sure enough, as I stepped away from the *biglietteria* and headed the few steps toward dock *numero quattro*, there on the horizon was the *Don Paolo* pulling into port. Before me, on the top deck, exchanging directions with *il capitano* on a walkie-talkie, was my man, or at least I hoped he was my man.

He was happy to see me and explained that he had not had time to *ricarica* his cell phone in order to text me. That happens a lot here. Why don't Italians subscribe on a monthly basis so they don't always have to *ricarica* at the *tabaccheria*?

I have learned that Italians really go out of their way to complicate life. They want to live stress free but they produce so much of their own stress that it becomes the music they sing in their animated way of communicating. Their hands are like a conductor's baton, waving notes hither and thither in a symphony of *allora* and *va bene*.

The trip takes an hour to cross to Ischia, giving us just enough time to reconnect without making him overly burdened. Yet, something was different today, he was lighter, we were happier. He actually held my hand, playing as our fingers mingled. They were still a perfect fit. I never knew I could hold a wish in my hand until Rocco held mine.

A souvenir t-shirt from London and a boobs lollipop brought a simple smile to his face and the urge to brag to the crew. It was getting easier. I could hear him telling them my name in Italian. I was headed toward the beach but this new light made my day brighter.

Ischia, for me, will always be magical, not to mention that it has the best beaches on the Bay of Naples. They are sandy and clean, not like the rocky shores which the locals are so used to on the main land.

Ischia is romantic in its isolation. It may be the largest of the Flegrean Islands but it's the smallest in tourist popularity. Those who do travel to its shores come "for the cure," to soak in its natural, volcanic, thermal hot springs. Then there are those of us who know that the "hottest" place to soak is in a private plunge pool at *L'Albergo Regina Isabella*...but I digress. I must stay in the present to move forward. Looking back only causes you to trip.

Vita in il momento. That will be my new motto.

This day would be my happy beach day. I took the Number Two bus to Poseidon Gardens and found a little spot in paradise. An explosion of natural color greets you from the minute you enter this thermal Garden of Eden. *Il giardineri* of Poseidon are a carpet of reds, pinks and yellows. The scent is heavenly and most newcomers are left speechless amid the flurry of picture taking in the floral beds. I dare you not to be happy amid such beauty.

There is a rivulet of steaming hot thermal water which trickles along the paths. The little gurgle is the white noise which puts you in a happy place. It's like the yellow brick road for grown-ups.

Sure, I could have a massage and dip in the mineral rich pools. Instead, I head *sempre dritto* to a spotless, quiet beach. There is the sand, the small waves, and of course, the cute lifeguard. Did you forget? This is Italy! I can get used to this life. Patience happens automatically here.

"Losing My Senses to Find My Soul"

In this place I close my eyes, the stress and pain disappear.
The cries of disappointment don't reach the shore.
Here in this place, the din I cannot hear.

The taste of sadness is bitter on the lips,
But in this place, the salty air is sweetened by a cool breeze.

Disappointment cuts like a blade through the heart.
Yet, in this place, the burn is washed away.
In the shade of the day, refuge falls easy as the voice of a child.

The warmth of the sun caresses me.
With each breeze I awaken to chance.
Here, in this place, my heart can still dance.

I awaken as the waves break closer and I am whole.

This was the perfect beach day. Some people need noisy crowds and music to enjoy the beach. All I need is a good book and the lapping of the waves.

I made my way back to the *porto*. The bus arrived early, allowing me time to stroll the coast. I bought a *caffè di nonno*, which is a cross between an iced cappuccino and *mocha gelato*, and grabbed a piling on the pier for a sit-down. It must've been an hour that I sat there, watching two young boys spend their time with their dream of a boat.

The tired rowboat looked more like a nightmare, full of seaweed, dead fish and debris but it was an adventure for this pair of mini *uomini*. They tossed out the ripe, dead fish which were floating in mucky water. Then they began scooping the mud with two oars. This is their day, their dream in the sun. Today they do not have a worry in the world but I wonder what their tomorrow will be like.

For now, it is enough to clean this boat...to make it their own...to row off into the unknown on this gloriously, sunny day.

As for me, I didn't know whether Sir Rocco would be my ride back across the bay but I was hopeful and said a little prayer. Sure enough, it was "the big ferry that could" on the horizon. It entered Ischia Porto only about ten minutes late, which in Italy, means just about on time.

He told me that he took a beach break for thirty minutes in Sorrento this afternoon. His bronze six-pack still makes my heart do ripples. Again, we sat and talked and planned a Sunday night rendezvous on his new *moto*. I was giddy with anticipation and he knew it, smiling his little boy grin. There is nothing on the planet more romantic than riding on the back of a *moto* through the hills, high on love and life, holding onto the one sure thing in your life or exhilarating in its uncertainty.

Dance class on Tuesday and again we started talking about him working in New York. He wants to wait another two or three years until he perfects his cooking skills.

First it was his English. Now it's his skills as a *pizzaiola*. Will he ever leave the nest? *Mamma mia*, how did I wind up with a *mammone*?

Rocco waits for perfection and nothing in life is ever perfect. I think part of the happiness which comes from any journey is enjoying the mistakes along the way. They are what make each opportunity uniquely your own.

We play some more...he is still holding my hand. Now, we are joking, teasing about the surprises which await him in the bedroom and the toys which I bought in London. When we get stuck on a word, we use my translator app and move on. It is not that we have ignored what happened, it is that we have learned from it and are moving forward.

He is moving at his own pace and I am finally comfortable with that...*pacienza, Lisa, molto pacienza.*

He is fascinated, playing with my iPad, as we see Marina Piccola and Sorrento approaching. It is a view that is in his soul. His father and his grandfather before him worked this port. In fact, *Nonno* lived in the red brick house which still stands at the end of the dock. This is Sorrento. This is home to Rocco.

"*Noi stiamo tornando a casa,*" he types into the translation app.

"*Questa era una bella giornata,*" he types again.

Si, si, yes it was.

"Un Respiro di Mio Cuore"

Non posso più respire senza di te.

Un sentimento unico per me.

Per il tempo, per lo spazio, ti sento.

Mi senti anche?

Tu sorride illumine la mia anima.

La passione del mio cuore

è una tempesta che non ha limiti.

Andiamo, piano, piano,

essere sensibili a durare per sempre.

Tu sei il un respiro di il mio cuore.

Chapter 11 - Uomini Italiani

*T*here is an old saying, "When everyone else says give up, hope whispers give it one more try."

I did not know what to expect when I set forth on this journey, walking away from a virtually dead legal practice for two months was the easy part. Getting started in a new land, with a new language, in a place that held so many memories of my life with Rocco, that was difficult beyond belief.

Sorrento is a lovely place but without work, without friends, without the conveniences of modern American life to entertain and numb the soul, it is living outside of my comfort zone on a grand scale. So, while I have been overwhelmed in sadness by the loss of my connection to Rocco in this place, it is giving me strength to evaluate what I truly need and want in life.

Spring is a wonderful time on the Sorrentine Peninsula and the Amalfi Coast. I make the distinction because there is an elite air to those who live here who are eager to tell you that the Amalfi Coast is from *Positano* to *Vietri sul Mare*, while Sorrento is on a separate peninsula.

Hey, I was never good at geography. As long as they all look onto the Bay of Naples, then it's all one coast to me.

As I sit here, the *Tramontana* continue to howl down from the Lattaris. The glint of sunlight caresses the orange and lemon groves outside my window, while the grey mist hovers on the mountaintops.

The rains are worse at night. The gusts swirl and the rain comes in sheets as I hide under the comforter, longing for central heating. The only thing which would make this villa apartment *tutto perfetto* would be a fireplace with the muscular descendant of a Roman god to keep me warm.

I've decided that Italian men are basically eye candy and nothing more. They stroll the piazzas like the cocks of the walk because that is what they are...followed by girls whose only ambition is to deliver *un pompino* (presidential sex) or *sesso* in the back of a car with the hope of getting pregnant and hence married. What a life!

I know that I am painting with a broad brush but Italian news reports that among young people in the south, unemployment is at 39% this April. Dozens of them sit around the street, all day, aimlessly, smoking dope and shopping. At night, it's dancing in clubs and sex in the back of a car. There is no motivation to change and apparently no encouragement from their parents to improve and get out of the house. The parents are actually enabling them by providing funds for their habits.

Of course, there are exceptions and I have met many wonderful people here, but my perception of the young population is what mystifies me. Equally as baffling are their perceptions or misconceptions of Americans, whom many envy and chide and treat rudely. Yet, each one of them has no qualms about asking any American for a job so they can move to the United States. They seem to think we're all rich here and some are not polite enough to hide their resentment.

One day, I lost my bearings on Via degli Aranci. I knew my destination was within spitting distance of where I stood but couldn't figure whether to turn right or left.

"*Scusa, Signora,*" as I approached an elderly shop-keeper with the face of stale bread.

The *malocchio* was alive and well in her eyes, as she stood with a younger woman. Neither of whom wanted to help this *straniera*.

They were about to send me 20 minutes in the wrong direction when my internal New York radar impelled me to cross the street to Mr. Eye Candy on his *moto*. Funny, his directions were just a half block to the left. Less than 5 minutes from where we stood…and in the opposite direction!

I turned and smiled knowing full well that *Signora Stale Bread* and her young counterpart were staring daggers at me. I smiled and waved to them, wondering about the source of their jealousy and venom.

I cannot imagine any New Yorker intentionally giving a tourist wrong directions. If these women are under the misconception that we want to steal their men, as Rocco has suggested to me, let me put their minds at ease. Give me someone stamped "Made in the U.S.A." any day. Remember, candy is dandy but some you should chew up and spit out before it rots your insides!

I must develop patience. It is difficult to imagine that this nurturing woman, *uh*, that would be me, who cared for four aging and frail relatives, has no patience but it is true. I think it's the realization of the brevity of life coupled with the fact that part of my family name translates to "it's fast," may have something to do with it. Lord, I hope it doesn't translate to "she's fast." That's all I need in the land of *vino* and *uomini*.

So, let's talk about men since that's what brought me here. I stopped asking female friends for advice just about the time I entered law school and changed my thought patterns forever. Women suck at giving advice. If you want to get inside a man's head, then ask another man, a straight man. They rarely pull punches and tell you, almost like a movie script, how the scene will unfold...even when I asked American guys about Italians. *Although my guy friends will tell you Rocco is a movie script unlike any they've ever memorized!* After all, men are men, in want of sex and food and ego gratification in whichever order is the easiest.

Men want it fast and easy. Now, you can apply that to many areas and it still works. Women - fast and easy. Work - fast and easy. Food - fast and easy. Conflict resolution...well, do you see where I'm going here? We women complicate to the point of total obfuscation. Why is that?

I readily admit that law school changed that thought process in me, in part. I no longer have time for nonsense. I do not have time for drama and I want everything fast and easy. So, that doesn't bode well for the patience skill set, does it?

I do have patience for advance planning a travel itinerary for a client or myself. So, with well-honed concierge skills, I set about researching Italian dating sites in advance of my journey of rediscovery.

It is like Sodom and Gomorrah in virtual Italy, I tell you. This truly is the land of humping and jumping, at least in the south. The funny thing is that many of the men use photos of famous Italian actors or soccer players as their profile photos. They go so far as to use many photos of their chosen celebrity alter ego, hoping that some unknowing women will believe that they are really that good looking and want to be raptured by them on the spot. *Mamma mia,* get real!

Here is where you come if you want a quick fix, an easy affair. Remember, that's how Rocco and I started. Southern Italian men see it as their duty to bed as many women as possible, right up to the sound of the death knell. Northern Italian men think the same way but are more refined in how they approach the situation.

It starts when they invade your space. They have this disarming way of approaching you and when they are within inches of your no-fly zone, their eyes pierce right through you, making you feel as if you have just been raptured without ever disrobing. They all do it. I think that's why many

Italian girls have mastered the bitch-approved, nose-in-the-air walk, as a way to put off these drooling men. Either that or it's because the girls are all trying to figure out whether they are the *fidanzata* or the *amante*, but we'll get to that!

Piano, Piano.

I did warn you early on that they are just eye candy. Now, I don't profess to be an expert on Italian lovers but I have had my share. Rocco aside, they leave a lot to be desired. In plain English, they've got no game. It's so sad. Their talent ends at the one-liners and their bedroom moves resemble something between a roadrunner and a jack-hammer. I have come to the realization that this can be blamed on two things - Italian porn and the country's small cars. The porn is awful and since they are accustomed to having sex on a car seat, it's done quickly just to get off and move on.

The emotional development of most men stops at 17 but at least American men become independent and develop really good game in bed. Not so much in Italy. They all make love like 17-year-old pubescent kids because that is all they are, emotionally and intellectually. They live at home. They have no real-life responsibilities and have sex in cars at 30, 40 and 50 years old. Their growth is stunted. Pun intended. Not to make this a steamy tale of erotica, which would clearly be an American tale, but Italian men have the staying power of about 30 seconds, a full minute if you're very, very lucky. I think it has to do with their tiny, roving den of iniquity.

Signor Snuggles, he was adorable in a pathetic sort of way.

"Lisa, why you say noooo?" He asked in his charming best English, while I tried to avoid his initial Italian advances.

OK, fast and easy, right?

Then, after our second or third time together, I asked why someone so cute didn't have a girlfriend.

"I do. Is this a problem for you?"

"No, but it's a big problem for you."

He still texts me, every now and then, thinking I'll weaken while in Sorrento. *Forza, Lisa, forza*!

At least he gets an A for honesty, sort of, and he is a cuddler.

Why can't they commit to just one woman? Flirting is an art form and fornication for them is just exercise. I remember Rocco telling me that he had many "friends" but none meant as much as I did because I was *his* woman and *the* most important girl in the world and he meant it. He told everyone that there was no one in the world like me.

So, was I the *fidanzata* or the *amante*? Again, we'll get to that distinction.

It's really not fair that God made so many of them so damn hot. It's a cruel joke. No matter their age, these men, for the most part, are breathtaking. Here in Sorrento, and especially on Capri, there are two kinds of men. There are the gorgeous, movie-star quality men who always display the latest fashion trend from Milan. Then there are the dark-eyed, oh my God, take your breath away, sun-kissed, muscular masterpieces. Here is where God came down and kissed the Earth, leaving behind an echo of beauty in both men and scenery.

I think it's a geographical phenomenon since all men here flirt more easily with women of all ages than they do in the north. The men are still magnificent in Tuscany or the Alps but you barely get a noticeable ogle when passing them on the street. Whereas in Rome, everyone is just too into themselves and city life to bother flirting.

Yet, here in Sorrento, even the tailor's pal, nearing 70, couldn't resist an old boy scout's try when I brought in jeans for alteration. The friend's eyes twinkled, as the tailor measured my bare waist.

"*Tu sei, mmm,*" waving his hands in a figure eight.

I was so proud just to make myself understood in Italian and they were so proud just to have a pretty girl in their men's tailor shop.

"*E quando*?" I ask, wanting to know when my altered pants would be ready.

"*In due giorni.*"

"*Da vero*?" I ask in disbelief, since it would likely take a week in New York.

"*Certo, quando tu sei bellissima, in due giorni.*"

Age does not matter here…to a point.

I've joined a local gym in an effort to make friends and find someone new to rapture me but I think it's the wrong gym. The average age is 18 and even I can't be that fast and easy!

Italian men generally think very little of women, seeing them as nothing more than sex objects except for mamma. *Certo*, because she only had sex once to conceive them. First Rocco and then *Signor Snuggles* who, last night, thought I would wait in the piazza until he finished a soccer match, whenever that might be. Do I look 18 and stupid or 50 and desperate? Think again, cowboy!

They believe women are at their disposal and simultaneously disposable. Their mothers are to blame, in large part, but so are the single women of Italy who let them get away with this abhorrent behavior. There are so many un-employed, sad, depressed people under 35 in the south that a cavalcade of shrinks could study here for a lifetime.

These days, sex, salsa and soccer occupy most of their time. Condom vending machines stand like sentries on eve-ry other corner, just down the block from makeshift shrines to the Virgin Mary. It's pretty funny considering that the Catholic Church dominates here and that's one institution which clearly frowns on premarital sex.

Guys and girls alike stroll past the condom machines; yet, they still bless themselves, making the sign of the cross, when they pass any roadside shrine to Mary. Maybe they should count their blessings since they pass the condom machines without ever using them, avoiding both disease and pregnancy, literally by the grace of God…or bless them-selves since most have seriously violated the Tenth Com-mandment, thou shall not commit adultery. No coveting!

Then again, maybe Italians really are closer to God. Let's ignore the fact that you cannot go one block anywhere in Italy without bumping into another church. There is also no distant mountain or hill without a cross on top.

You see the crosses everywhere, where the earth meets the sky. They sit like lightning rods, antennae that reach into the heavens just in case God has a special message. So, maybe Italians really are treated differently! Heavenly, isn't it?

I could not believe that one friend today just shrugged when Rocco's name came up.

"Neapolitan women don't expect fidelity," she said. So, does that make cheating acceptable? Yet, Rocco didn't cheat. He ended our relationship before he went to sow his wild oats in *Thailandia*.

My new strategy will be to try to think like an Italian man and see if that gets me any closer to understanding them. Let's call it a social experiment that both Margaret Mead and Alfred Kinsey would support wholeheartedly. First order of business is to give *Signor Snuggles* another at bat, if you pardon my analogy.

He apologized for ditching me for soccer. The sun is shining. This is *siesta* in Sorrento and it's time to play.

We start with pizza. What else but that food naturally leads to lust, and I find out that the girlfriend is really his roommate of ten years.

"So, how would you feel if she has another man?" I ask, really wanting some insight. He just shrugs his shoulders as if to care less and with the knowledge and confidence that it would never happen.

"Seriously, why do you do it?" I am thinking that women everywhere, especially his roomie, would like to know.

The answer is priceless. "Because I am an Italian man," he says with a sheepish grin and proud of his boorish behavior.

"That's such bullshit and bloody ridiculous." Yet, here I go again for a lunch time sex fest, trying to block the boredom and loneliness which I can't shake free.

"So, you like-uh di sex with me?" Really, boys, if you have to ask, just take a guess at the answer.

"Oh, God, are we there yet?" whizzed through my head. Yet, I don't have the heart to tell *Signor Snuggles* that I'm bored. So, I offer a noncommittal grin, thinking very much like a man and now seemingly acting like one. Hey, whatever works. Research answers and my emotional void are still left unfulfilled.

La Lingua di Amore

Growing up as an Italian-American, in a strong Sicilian-Calabrese family, and having studied the Italian language with a "northerner from Milan," I was taught that there are always a million ways to say one thing in Italian, everything from telling someone to sod off (sorry for the British reference) to saying I love you.

In Italian there are two verbs, *amare* which means to love and *volere* which means to want...not to mention the word *innamorata* which means in love. In the good old U.S.A., we only have one four-letter L-word, "love." It's the word everyone hates to say first; the word everyone clearly knows the meaning of, no matter how many different degrees we assign to it; the word that is clearly different from the other L-word of lust. Oh, I have been in lust many, many times...and in love many times. I knew the difference each time, well, maybe not but we only use one word for the ultimate human emotion - love.

In the school of life, in the classroom of my family, I was told there was a distinct difference between the Italian use of *ti amo* and *ti voglio bene*. I was always led to believe that the use of the phrase "*ti voglio bene sai,*" when used between a man and a woman, is much more heartfelt, much more passionate, much more "*la lingua d'amore*" than the trite "*ti amo.*" I was told this by my grandparents who were married for more than 60 years (talk about love!). I was told this by my mother who is the singular, most romantic and most passionate woman on the planet, someone who changed religions for love! So, how come TVB has become so complicated for the people who ooze romance and passion from their first breath? Yes, that's right. They even shorten it for texting to TVB, rather than taking the time to write out a very important inference.

I think the answer lies in a clash between traditional customs and modern practicalities. Traditionally, Italians put too much pressure on their children to marry the "right" person. Traditionally, Italians, rooted in an obsessive allegiance to old-school Catholicism, believe that if you *fare l'amore* then certainly you must marry that person or you will forever be a blemish on *una famiglia*. Therefore, there is the nexus between *fare l'amore* and *amare* as the verb. This has led to many conflicted Italians, both young and old, who partake in *fare sesso* and use the trite "*TVB*" with everyone from their *fidanzata* to their beloved S.S.C. Napoli soccer team. Although, when it comes to S.S.C. Napoli, they will also use the English word "love" in an ironic turn of sport!

Further, many Italians who truly love each other would never dream of living together for fear of their families' opinions, let alone the parish clergy! So, this *straniera* believes they dumb down their feelings and use TVB, turning it more into an acronym for American "puppy love," because if they use *ti amo* then that means they're tripping down the aisle into an uncertain "married" future. Game over!

They have further complicated affairs by creating various labels for relationships that should simply be boyfriend-girlfriend; fiancé-fiancée; or husband-wife...and the lover.

What do you call that man you have been living with for three years without the benefit of marriage? *Mamma mia!* Or the man you have celebrated holidays with for the past four years? Or just the teenage boy next door whom your niece has been dating for six months? The answer is not that simple.

In the U.S., you are born and you have a boyfriend (OK, several dozen, but who's counting?). You get engaged once (OK, maybe twice because that first idiot was a *jadrool*). Then you get married.

It is simple – boyfriend, *jadrool*, fiancé, husband. In Italy, not so fast.

For three-and-a-half years I never knew what to call Rocco. I would introduce him as my boyfriend. He would call me his woman but introduce me as his friend. As for his family, they called me *"L'Americana,"* with affection, *certo.* Other men in Sorrento, who knew both of us, would tell me that after three-and-a-half years, I was definitely Rocco's *fidanzata,* no matter how he saw it, and so, the resulting confusion and *messaggi mista.*

Raggazzo is that special boy teenage girls "fall in love with," the one whose name they write on a padlock and toss the key into the bay, memorializing an eternal bond. It is their eternal lock of love. They should only know what wisdom age will bring them. Girls, well into their 30s, will waste too much silly time trying to lock a man with handcuffs, while the men continually rebel, avoiding the proverbial ball and chain.

Fidanzato is a boy who is much more committed to the relationship. He is the one you will marry, even if you are 17 and will not marry for another ten years.

Compagno is used for the man you live with in sin, without the benefit of marriage, although some would argue about any benefit to marriage!

Italians chide the American use of the word boyfriend by anyone over the age of 17. Perhaps it is because of the macho connotation of that boy versus man thing here in Italy.

They tell me that *fidanzato* is now used to mean boyfriend without an official betrothal. However, just try to sell that idea to an Italian man who clearly knows that he is not engaged and the woman who truly wants to be.

Or what about the couple in their 30s, 40s or 50s who is living together? Does the label for him as *un compagno* make him less committed to the relationship than someone who gives a woman a ring but who keeps her waiting for years?

Ah, then there is the *amante*. She is the lover that every Italian man has and keeps for afternoons or evenings full of passionate sex. He has a *fidanzata* or a *moglie* and an *amante*, maybe even two. This could go on for years. They juggle many balls in the air; yet, it's their balls which cause all of this grief.

This world is so tied up in labels and old world traditions which complicate the simplest of expressions of love. We raise or lower expectations depending on the culture and its related taboos instead of just going with your heart. When it comes to relationships, it should not matter what you call anyone. Only what two people know in their hearts to be true is the key.

Torino

So, with all of this linguistic baggage in tow, I journeyed north, to Torino, thinking men would be different there, since I had recently been made aware of the great social divide between the north and the south.

Northerners receive more education and better jobs than southerners, who rely mainly on tourism, creating this great socio-economic schism. Yet, when it comes to the thought patterns of Italian men, they are basically the same and there is absolutely nothing clear about how they express their emotions.

Torino's *Piazza Castello* has likely hosted debates on this, the greatest of life's mysteries, since the 16th century. It was the power base of the Dukes of Savoy and now serves as the stage, the grand boulevard of life, in this northern power base. However, I venture to say that not one solution has ever evolved over the centuries and many bottles of wine shared between friends.

"Please enlighten me," I ask Maurizio. "Tell me the difference between when an Italian man says "*ti amo*" and when he says "*ti voglio*." I implore my well educated *amico*, at least clear on our relationship.

"*Ti amo* is only used to express the deep love you feel for the woman you want to spend your life with and *ti voglio* is basically used when you lust for someone."

"What?"

It is quite clear to him, as he dismisses my parents' and grandparents' explanations and tells me that I should not expect to understand what only true Italians can express.

Really? I feel like telling him to *vaffanculo* but we wait patiently for our friend Marco to arrive because surely he will be much wiser and shed a different light on this discourse.

The question looms over us in this great space, on this sunny day, as Marco approaches, with an unknowing smile.

"Please tell her what *ti voglio* means," Mauri asks the new sage on the scene.

As I rise to greet him, Marco, meeting me for the first time, sweeps me up in a huge embrace and gives me *un abbraccione stretto* and laughs.

They explain that Italian is a very particular language, while I protest that love is love and that's so much easier.

The epiphany I received in *Piazza Castello* is that men today, especially Italian men, are so scared to admit love to a woman. They fear they will wind up a divorce statistic, supporting her forever because of Italy's archaic divorce laws and high marriage fatality rate. I speculate that many of them are definitely "in love" with the women in their lives but are hesitant to use the word *amore* lest it lead them down the aisle to a perceived state of monetary hell.

The three of us rise from this in-depth discussion to go for dinner. I think we have moved on for the night. Yet, as we head out, Marco taps me on the shoulder and with a wink in his eye says, "And then there is always *ti voglio bene*."

"That is when a man cares deeply for you and he wants to be a part of your life if you would honor him with your permission," Maurizio blabbers on and I am further perplexed.

Do you see why Italian men complicate something that should be so simple? They should stop looking at the basic emotion of love as an eternal investment in a family perception, or worse yet as a "lose-lose" economic proposition. Instead, no matter what your language or where you live, you should look at love as an experience to be cherished, no matter the degree, and stop trying to label it and stop trying to rationalize it.

Love comes. Love goes. And, when it takes your breath away...and it does...then hold on and don't fear the ride of a lifetime. So, *ti amo o ti voglio bene* should not be the question. It should be the answer!

Ma, gli uomini di tutto il mundo, they should all come with warning labels tattooed to their foreheads, you know the kind that come with pillows, warning of impending doom until removed by the new owner. Women would then be able to add notes in an invisible ink seen only by subsequent lovers. Truly, it would be the ultimate unwritten code shared between women!

Chapter 12 - To the Mountaintop

*T*he view of *Vesuvio* from the terrace is stunning. I can see this sleeping giant each morning as I start the day. Well, it's not quite sleeping, from what I've read and been told by the locals. So, it is with a bit of trepidation that I head out today to discover why this mighty mountain lures Napoletani like *Eloi* to a higher power.

I first noticed the power of *Vesuvio* with Rocco. Each time we would pass the coast he would say, "Look, Napoli," as if it was his first time. Yet, this continued day after day, night after night, for several years. "Look, Napoli."

Then I noticed the behavior of adults on the train. As they circumnavigate *Vesuvio*, adults stare at it in silent awe, as the train chugs along. It is a site they have seen each day of their entire lives but they are in a trance as it looms on the horizon. Children, on the other hand, unaware of the true, massive thermal energy of this mountain, are full of delight and wonder.

"Mamma, Vesuvio, guarda, Mamma!"

It's a volcano. It's deadly. It can blow at any moment. So, why am I climbing it today?

I decided to rent a car for the journey, not wanting to be limited by the time constraints of a tour bus. I figure conquering a volcano on my own will be quite empowering, once I get there.

The sun is shining and I am prepared with water and layers of sweaters. Rocco warns me to grab the climbing stick at the volcano's entrance and I laugh thinking it's a mountain, how steep could it be. Hey, I grew up in New York City. What do we know of climbing mountains?

The first challenge is to navigate my way to *Parco Nazionale del Vesuvio*, since I will need to drive through Pompei and that poses a challenge for anyone with a GPS. There is some sort of polar pull when the GPS hits the perimeters of Pompei, throwing the magnetic and satellite references into a whirlwind of miscalculations. It's like the Bermuda Triangle of Italy. I can't figure it out but it frustrates me each and every time. Thankfully, I am now familiar enough with driving the A3 to use my internal compass and after a few circles around the city, I am on my way.

This is going to be easy, I think to myself, not realizing that *Vesuvio* is about 4200 feet above sea level, give or take a few inches and depending whom you ask. The dizzying drive is making me nervous and my acrophobia is kicking in. There is no one with me to assuage my fear and no one who even knows where I am should the car go flying off the mountain.

Stay focused, Lisa. Look at the road ahead, not sideways, not back, just keep moving forward and you'll be alright.

My emotional fortitude keeps pushing me in the right direction.

I am halfway there and the thought of giving up looms heavy in the air conditioned car. Yes, it is hot today. Yes, I am nervous but there is nowhere to turn around.

Surely, the observation station at the halfway point will be sufficient, though the site of busloads of students is enough to scare me off that path and I continue the ascent. I was mentally exhausted as my car pulled into the crowded parking lot.

The line at the ticket window numbered at least fifty and it was much colder here. The sun was shining but this outpost felt like the North Pole. Three layers of sweaters with shorts and sneakers just weren't going to cut it on the volcano and I still had a long way to journey. OK, I was looking for any excuse not to make this climb.

Forza, Lisa, forza. You can do this.

My lawyer brain kicks in and I soon realize that the likelihood of this intelligent woman making this steep drive in a car is not likely to happen again too soon, so I might as well endure for the climb of a lifetime. This trip is challenging my inner resolve on so many levels.

Sure enough, as Rocco promised, two men stood at the ready, dispensing alpine walking sticks for hundreds of intrepid and ill-prepared tourists. My inner day-tripper surfaced along the way, snapping one breathtaking panorama after another, posing my doll at the edge of the volcano, bothering other wayfarers to take photos of me. I was slowly turning into a popsicle. It was 80 degrees and sunny in Sorrento. What the hell happened up here? Maybe I was in hell, arctic hell.

I had landed on another planet in another time. The surface was alien, rough and rocky in many shades of ugly grey and brown, instead of lush like the coast, with blues and greens. The most disconcerting thing was the smoke which emanated along the way. *Vesuvio* is far from dead. It's still blowing off steam and determined scientists cling to the cliff, as if Velcro-ed to this giant, waiting for something to happen.

In true Italian fashion, tiny red vehicles, *vigili del fuoco*, are parked every 100 meters or so. I laugh to myself, as if the Italians really believe that these small sentinels could do anything if *Vesuvio* decides that this is the day to make history.

And make no mistake, it is not if *Vesuvio* will blow again, as it did in 79 A.D., burying Pompei, or as it did the last time it was angry in 1944, during World War II, killing some 28 people. It is only a matter of when it will erupt again and I truly pray that it is not today.

Experts say the smoke which rises is a good thing. It lets *Vesuvio* vent, as we all need to do, and without such venting it would explode. *Giorno per giorno*, it will give one day!

Making it to the mountaintop is an exercise in both physical and mental stamina for someone with a fear of heights. It's just me and my stick and a mountain full of strangers. The cappuccino stands along the way fortify my ability to carry on, up and then down. I did it. I climbed to the mountaintop and lived to tell the tale, albeit skidding along gravel at a few passes.

There are 5,000,000 people who live in Naples and some 600,000 of them live on its outskirts. Signs at the entrance say *"Vesuvio, the father who kills his son!"* OK, now, it's starting to sink in why the locals stare in awe. It's a force not to be reckoned with in a country which has not revised its evacuation plan in more than twenty years.

Maybe it will be time to go home soon. Funny though, when I returned to the villa tonight, simultaneously exhausted and energized, the skeleton key turned the lock at the first try.

Chapter 13 - Amici Miei

had come here not expecting to feel the deep sense of isolation which shrouded me during the early, rain-soaked stages of this odyssey. In hindsight and sunlight, I now realize that relationships don't happen, without effort, on any level.

As a foreigner in a strange land, I could not bluster upon the scene and expect everyone to greet and love me. My New York sensibility had to relax into this new life. I had to assimilate to life with a *siesta*.

I longed to reach out and grab this world by its *limoncellos* but this world moves at a much slower pace. You cannot thrust yourself upon a new culture. You must grow into it.

Here, I do not have the purpose work gives me, the direction it gives me to get out of bed each morning. It becomes the social linchpin by which we are connected to others. In the absence of a job, it is difficult to build social connections, especially as an adult. As children, we go to school and we just start talking to each other. As adults, we erect walls for protection, which also limits our access to new opportunities.

If you think back to your childhood and the first special friends who entered your life, I imagine none of them were instant. Sure, you met other kids on those first tenuous days of school but it took a few weeks of daily contact before you developed that "best friend" rapport.

I have some American expat friends here in the south, in Calabria and Salerno, but in the south of Italy, that might as well be a different country and just as difficult to get to. So, I had to let go of the safety net of relationships and trust that the road ahead would manifest new experiences.

As this new lightness of my being yielded to the nuances of Italian life, I launched each day on a new landscape, promising myself to live in the moment and trying to understand the joy that can bring. Then, when you relax and allow yourself to enjoy these pleasures, a new life starts to take shape in and around you, and relationships begin to happen on their own, effortlessly!

I read somewhere that it helps to make friends in the local shops and markets in these small villages. It gives you a sense of belonging because it is a constant and everyone has to eat, right?

I have been eating healthier since leaving New York. I am cooking more and making frequent trips to the *supermercato*. I balance the carbohydrates with frequent trips to my new gym. There is just one problem. Bar Rita stands between the villa and the gym and it's usually lunch or dinner time when I am on my way home after a workout. Life isn't fair sometimes.

At first I tried the *arancini* and *polpette di melanzane*, then the *cannoli con cioccolato*. I figure I can indulge since I must climb a hill of Vesuvian proportion back to the villa.

Always there with a smile to greet me is Imma. She has become my enabler, she smiles and I eat. It's a beautiful friendship built around food, as are most things in Italy.

It's funny, now, that I think about it. I was like Goldilocks trying to find a new gym that was just right. The first was way too small and the fitness director insisted that I do sets his way and not run a circuit. Yeah, sell that somewhere else. The second was too snooty, staffed by Surrentina who see American women as the enemy and not very welcoming. Now, the third gym, that was just right.

It is smack dab in the middle of town, just off the piazza and full of friendly staff, albeit the other male members have yet to leave puberty. I exercise there at least three times a week, always to DJ Radio, and realize that I have a fitness anthem that suits this entire journey.

"*This is a Part of Me*" by Katy Perry plays at least twice during an hour-long session and the more I hear it, the more I realize how the lyrics fit my new world order.

I defy anyone to describe my spirit as anything but generous but after being stepped on by people I thought were friends and family, generosity goes out the window. The strength of my independent core is now firmly rooted in self-reliance.

We each journey through this life only once. We alone must live with our choices and decisions. If we have not hurt anyone along the way, then we have done well. It is our judgment which defines us; yet, we should not judge others for we each need to learn our own lessons along the way.

"*No, no, no signora, non così. Prova come questo,*" as the fitness trainer assesses my form on the lat machine.

A helping hand is offered and my form is upright and just where it should be.

"*Grazie.*"

His watchful eye pans the room as I move to the adductor machine and sure enough, again, I receive a helping hand.

"*Mamma mia,*" I cry out, as he increases both intensity and spread on the machine, pushing me to tighter thighs.

"It is better?" he smiled, in the little English he knows.

True, you may get free towels and soap and iced water in a New York gym but the fitness trainers only help when you pay them. In Sorrento, we barely get one roll of toilet paper to get us through the week in the locker room and soap is a novelty altogether.

Italians may rough it when it comes to the gym and to daily life, but they help when it matters. I would much prefer someone who has my back than the *accouterment* which goes with people caught up in the shallowness of socialization without the fortitude of true friendship. Toilet paper, on the other hand, is a bare necessity and quite cheap, *per favore*!

Forza, Lisa, forza…this is getting much easier.

School, home and work are the three most common places to meet and make new friends and I am fortunate enough that my work is now taking me into the unknown. I enter eager and awaken to new experiences without the rose-colored vacation glasses of tourists.

I am making progress in this new life with each step out the front gate. My Italian is improving and I am now at the point where Italians are approaching me for directions and when I respond, they seem to understand and thank me.

Carmine, the *sarto*, is also a great help. He is a real friend besides a fantastic tailor. I often catch him sitting outside for an afternoon espresso break. A five-minute stop turns into a two-hour-long conversation in Italian.

Carmine's kindness affords me the security I need to practice my Italian on a daily basis. We have now moved from *"buon giorno"* to great discussions about life and men.

"Ascolta me, Lisa, per favore, ascolta me," he pleads with me to steer clear of young Italian men, thinking that as a lawyer, a well-educated woman, I deserve much better.

I understand his old school beliefs but do not believe that education should be the great socio-economic divide between people who care for each other. As my *Nonno* always told me, "the heart wants what the heart wants." Be happy with whoever makes your heart "palpitate" is what he would tell me.

Another expat friend suggested I have a party and invite everyone I have met along the way. That may work in the desert where she is stationed but not in Sorrento. Italians don't make plans. They will tell you we have to *organizzano.* Organize? Really? Italians don't organize. They debate. They talk loudly. But they certainly don't organize.

You can ask almost any Italian if they want to go for a coffee, for lunch, for a drink, maybe two, three, four times and each time they will tell you *a presto!* Then, the day before you are returning to America, they say, "Are you free for a coffee?" That's their problem. They wait and wait, and think and think, but never do until too much time has passed and then it's too late.

Basta organizzare.

Vivete la vostra vita adesso, altrimenti non succede nulla. Capito?

Roma Ancora

Every once in awhile, without any grand design or plan, magic happens without much organization. You meet a special person. You visit a special place. You feel like Cinderella for a day. For me, in Rome, photographer Rochelle Cheever made all of that happen.

Rochelle was one of the many contacts I had come to know during the past several years as a travel journalist and concierge. So, when she heard the stress and despair of my broken heart across cyberspace, she suggested that a photo shoot would put me just right. As soon as I could make another escape from Sorrento, we were to rendezvous in Rome where girls can always get into trouble together. She suggested that my first stop be *Noi Salon.* I was already loving my new BFF.

In Italian, the word *noi* translates to we. In Rome, it literally means the difference between OK and WOW! These guys spoke my language, literally and figuratively. Partners Rick, Massimo and Giuseppe are one-third American and two-thirds Neapolitan and totally tuned into me.

Finding them was no easy feat. I needed a secret password and clues to decipher in order to locate this hidden treasure in Rome's ancient *Piazza del Popolo.* It was so covert and CIA-like. There was a tiny brass plaque and an even smaller buzzer, hidden in plain sight, and the voice from Oz granted me access behind the large, iron gate. There is no man behind the curtain but these guys are definitely the wizards.

After four hours on yet another tortuous bus ride from Sorrento, Massimo whisked me into the washing station faster than I could say, "use your magic wand!" Add to that an hour in the hands of Federico's magic make-up chair and I was ready for my close-up.

They primped me. I inhaled the attention and for the first time since leaving New York, I was finally with men who "got me."

Dressing up was a hoot. Rochelle had prepped me from across the ocean and I took a suitcase full of "extras" just to make sure, because a girl can never have enough of anything on dress-up day!

Rochelle orchestrated the shoot in and around *Piazza del Popolo*. I jumped from fountain to doorway, from hotel rooftop to side alley, with the agility of an ingénue in stilettos on cobblestone streets. As for Rochelle, she did what she does best, creating a world of beautiful dreams through her viewfinder.

For hours we played, running through the Piazza, to the artsy district of Via Margutta, through the ancient side-streets near the Tiber River, from steps off the beaten path to borrowing a parked *moto*, bicycle and even an old door knocker, as props.

I felt like a starlet on a Hollywood shoot in Rome. Men checked me out, as I sauntered past in heels and sunglasses and a big, floppy hat, and children giggled as Rochelle shouted directions to me like a female Fellini.

I have traveled the world and still find Rome to be the most romantic city. I have spent a career on radio and TV, in front of the camera, and I learned a long time ago that how well you look has a lot to do with the creative team which helps you in the spotlight.

In my travels around this crazy world, I have found few people as special as Rochelle Cheever. She is not only an inspiring photographer but an angel as well. I will forever see Rome in a new light thanks to her.

Each day I am learning something new about relationships, be they man or woman, friend or family. I find my happiness where I choose to. No one can give it to me. What one person can do for another is share a life experience which hopefully yields joy for both hearts. It's a syncopated rhythm which pulsates through our lives, pulling us to and fro, from one experience to the next.

For a long time my joy, as a woman, came from giving to others. I gave to the men in my life way more than they gave to me, either emotionally or spiritually. My bad relationship pattern was nothing if not consistent. I truly believed that love could conquer all. I thought that if I had enough love for two people then I could fix them or fix us but that is not how good energy is supposed to flow back and forth.

As women, we often fall into this pattern of doing and giving without taking or receiving nearly enough to nurture our own being. It happens from when we're young. We are taught to play with dolls and be the Mommy and take care of them. These skills are not bad but they are passed down over generations, from woman to woman, and we are not taught how to take what we want.

Men, on the other hand, are taught to set their sight on the goal, on the endgame, and fight for what they desire. Fathers teach sons how to win. That is what they do - win a ballgame, win at business, win the girl they want to marry and fight like hell until they reach their goal. They battle to the finish line and then they move forward, onto the next.

I am at a point in life where I have given a lot to many, many people. There were the men I thought I could fix and then continued to languish for long after the finish line. There were the friends I gave more trust to than they deserved because they were the takers. There were the relatives I gave my heart to only to realize that a syncopated rhythm does not necessarily flow between people who share a bloodline.

Allora, I am approaching life differently now. My happiness may come from giving to others when I can see the joy and sense of appreciation flow back in my direction.

It is giving in a different way. It is bestowing love and feeling satisfied in the joy that brings to another life. It is a synergistic ebb and flow that should yield enough positivity to course as a life force between two beings to sustain them.

Relationships take work. We are not gods. We cannot generate energy on our own. We were created to work together, to fill gaps in our own energy field by revitalizing each other. It is love, through acts of human kindness, which recharges our souls. However, if at some point that energy only moves in one direction, it drains its source while recharging the receiver.

This is how women who love too much interact with men. It also applies to some girlfriends we always call to vent; to share; to enjoy. They never seem to pick up the phone first. This goes on for years until we realize that the friendship is truly one-sided.

It also applies to the relatives you always help because "they're family" until you realize that blood does not always bind you in a symbiotic, synergistic relationship. You help and help but when you ask for assistance, they do not reciprocate. There are some of those people in every family.

This is how stress wears you down. The pressure of caring for everyone but you is draining. At first, your adrenaline kicks in and you work even harder to try to make someone contribute as much as you are to the relationship or you do more than your share to compensate for the lack of doing on their part. That is the first red flag.

Then you begin to tire since your energy field has weakened. You tire of the daily routine. Yet, you begin to tolerate negativity from the other person because they continue to benefit and the energy is clearly flowing one way. For some, this takes a physical toll and you can wind up needing medical or psychological care because you are frayed like a well-worn doormat, always there, ever-obliging but never nurtured. This is the second red flag.

Eventually, someone leaves the relationship and you are left wondering what happened. It's a vicious cycle that we givers repeat, over and over again, until we see the light. Often it's a glimmer at the end of a long, dark tunnel, or it can be sudden onset awareness. However it happens, there is no turning back once you have achieved this epiphany. It is time to seize the day and be selfish, for want of a better word.

People leave. They die. They walk away or they fade into your past. After you survive the shock and grieve the loss, you realize that there is more, free heart-space inside of you. There is more time in the day for you to pursue what makes you happy in the short time that we each have to chase that dream.

Each day is a gift. While life takes work, it is yours to make great.

Think about it. It takes effort to enjoy a day in the sun, to let your mind and cares go and soak in its warmth. Stare at the horizon and get lost, as a cool breeze wafts by with the lightest hint of coconut oil.

In this age of digital everything, life is crowded with the white noise of devices. It takes concentrated effort to leave that world behind to enter the realm of relaxation and focus on the inner you.

What is your joy? It is yours to give. It is so much extra effort to convince someone else to give it to you. It is so much extra effort to wait for someone else to make you smile when smiling is so easy.

The point is that life, your life, is worth the effort. It is worth it from the moment you wake until the second you dream of things to come tomorrow. Waiting for someone else is the lazy route to nowhere.

Surrender to your dreams and let them launch your tomorrow. Start to think and do like a man and fight for what you want until you reach your goal.

There's an esoteric philosophy that you can change your stars at the moment of your solar return each year. For the astrological uninitiated, the solar return happens each year around your birthday and is so marked by the sun being at the exact same degree in the sky as it was at the moment of your birth. It is a return to your "original" position, your celestial home.

The stars and planets will appear differently depending on where you are in the world. So, if you change your geographic location, you can literally "change your stars" and plot your course for the year ahead.

Now, despite having spent my last birthday in the arms of the man I love on an incredibly romantic weekend escape, being in Sorrento did not set my course for success.

So, with psychic compass at the ready, I set my star chart for Venice and figure this coming year can only get better.

Venice

As I flew over Venice, I noticed that it is a city on the edge of history, its own history. It is on the brink of sinking into the very waters which give it life. As we neared Marco Polo Airport, I could not help but be overwhelmed by the amount of the city which is already underwater. Whole streets have given way to the sea. It is a modern day Atlantis.

There has been an upswing in seismic activity in the north of Italy this year and this week's earthquakes rumbled the city's already precarious position in Italy's future. Thousands of years of culture are in jeopardy.

The Venetians are a stark contrast to Napoletani. Here they are neither aloof nor phony. They are Venetians without apology to anyone. This is their home and they barely tolerate the thousands of tourists who infest their city of canals like barnacles, clinging to someone else's dock.

The water laps outside my window on the Grand Canal, as church bells echo in the distance. My room has a Murano glass chandelier with little pink flowers and matching sconces. It is nine minutes past midnight and while I wasn't born in this time zone, I am in Venice and it is my birthday. Life is good.

The rain clouds my first full day in this romantic place but Venice does not hold back. It gives and gives until you are captured by its allure.

Venice draws you in like a vintage spy movie from the 1940s. It is shrouded in a mist that is neither heavy nor oppressive but envelops the city so that it does not give up its secrets too easily. In that respect, Venice is like a beautiful, confident woman. It is at once mysterious and exposed.

I stroll through *Piazza San Marco*, long after the crowds have left, and listen as the anchored gondolas bob up and down and the raindrops glisten on the pavement. I hear the strains of classical music coming from *Caffè Florian* and imagine dancing in the piazza, in the rain, with the right partner. There is something so Titanic-like about the spirit and ghosts which persist in Venice. It is hypnotizing.

There is a veiled, softness about Venice. There is nothing harsh about her. Where Rome is a truly masculine city, Venice is all feminine. It is as though you look at the horizon and there is a diffuser on the lens or a lace curtain across the window to its soul. She is pink and warm and tranquil...unlike Venetians who can be downright rude. I nearly fell over in today's morning rush hour at the bottom of the Rialto Bridge, as a senior citizen, annoyed by tourists in his path, purposefully pushed me out of his way.

"*Vaffanculo*, are you kidding me?" Time to go home. '*Torno a Sorrento.*

Leaving Venice today, there is a beautiful stillness at dawn over the city. Piazza San Marco shows no trace of thousands of tourists from the night before, not even garbage lines the streets. It is peaceful, stately, as it has been for hundreds of years.

I needed to navigate the back streets to the dock for my water taxi back to the airport. The bridge near the hotel was closed last night due to earthquake damage. As I happened upon the water's edge, the bouncing gondolas, shrouded in their blue sheaths, were the only sign of life besides the occasional pigeon.

I had wanted to take the same photo as *Nonna* had fifty years earlier, arms spread, pigeons all over her, enjoying life to the max. Yet, I am certain that she is shaking her head knowing full well that my Calabrese genes, at times, do not let the Sicilian joy and passion take over in my life. I see the pigeons as rats with wings, and in the fifty or so years since *Nonna* took her photo, I imagine the pigeons now carry superbugs. *Ewwww!*

I do not know if I will return to this city of water. I have truly enjoyed my short stay and I would like to think that one day I'll return. I learned, however, that I do not need a man to travel for romance. The myth of the romance we create, which we crave, lives inside our heads. What lives inside our soul is much more important and much more palpable if you would only give yourself permission to go there.

I turn *un angolo* for the taxi and approach the dock, fully expecting to see other luggage-laden tourists for the boat ride back to Marco Polo. However, I am pleasantly surprised to learn that it's just me. Me and Mattia.

Oh, *mamma mia*! I fantasize riding his backbone like a pony as we leisurely, quietly glide through the Grand Canal. He takes his time, slowly, patiently, enjoying this morning, explaining in Italian the sites along the way. He's at the helm and I am his first-mate, the morning breeze blowing through my hair with a mist on the horizon, as we near the Rialto Bridge. It is our moment to start the day and I feel like a movie star in a private motorboat with a Roman god in command. I am the star of my own life!

Venetian men are so different than Napoletani; yet, I must focus. I must remember that they are still Italians first and that means they are eye candy...but oh, what candy. Oh, so yummy! He doesn't need a gym. He tosses a rope to secure the boat and lifts luggage as though it were as light as a picnic basket.

His looks are not dark but lighter; yet, he's still Italian. *"Focus, Lisa."* Then, as we near the next dock, and reality wakens me to the fact that three old ladies are going to ruin my joy ride, I notice his keychain...it is a yellow beach shoe...*oh, Dio*, he can't be gay!

151

Venice is a city on a foundation of sand, quicksand. It takes only one day to notice shopkeepers who sweep water from their doorstep on a daily basis and pools of water in the middle of Piazza San Marco. It is sinking. I remember thinking how tragic as we flew in…now, as I leave, I think how tragic that this runway sits on sand, oh, dear Lord, up, up and away! I can't wait to get back to Napoli…*sono a casa nuova*.

So strange, when I finally returned to the villa, I entered the gates and I missed the rotting oranges. Someone had cleaned the garden in my absence and it was bare. Not to worry, they will again fall to the ground, silent in their dying leap and filling up the footpath.

I have finally found *sfogliatelle* heaven at Dolce e Gelato. It's the new kid on the block, literally, having opened on Corso Italia in the first week of May. After a month long search I found the perfect *sfogliatelle*. The blue-eyed barista, Davide is also easy on the eyes and a nice way to start the morning. He always stencils a cocoa happy face onto my cappuccino.

"Don't forget my happy face today. *Oggi è ultimo colazione, primo ritorno a New York.*" I remind him, although it was unnecessary.

Davide, *con occhi blu*, places the cup just so I can see the happy face. "He is happy too because he can start the day having breakfast with you," he says. How can you not love this place?

After breakfast, I stroll through the Piazza one last morning. Sorrento is *perfetto* in the morning before all of the tourists wake up and crowd the narrow streets.

I stroll down to Marina Piccola and the tiny, public beach just to the left of Peter's Beach. A group of irksome teens has cut class for a morning swim to take advantage of this delightful day. The water is clear, right to the bottom of this rocky shore. It lacks sand, so it's rarely cloudy unless summer debris trashes the shoreline.

I dip my toes in the cool water of the bay. My shadow swirls at my feet, reminding me of the ever-changing ebb and flow of my time here.

When I arrived, I was lost. My spirit had gone grey and my soul was sad. This place rejuvenates me. It took time and will continue to do so. Life is a journey, *giorno per giorno*.

I end my day on the terrace, surrounded by the beauty of endless orange and lemon groves framed by the distant mountains. The city is at my doorstep. I can hear the traffic and ambulances pass by but I can also hear the birds chirping and the constant, ping, pong, of the tennis balls across the net at the club next door.

Today, there are also the cries of a newborn. A new life began during my time here. What a fitting metaphor!

Chapter 14 - A Domani

It was in January that I counted the days until I left for Italy. Now, with just hours until I return home, I do not want to leave. I recall the first three chaotic and rainy weeks and the depression that held me in a vice. Now, those problems, as most in life, are not so grand.

Life and friends take time. Rarely do relationships of value happen instantly. I will make change happen when I return to New York.

Yet, how do I go back to life in New York? Life here is not perfect but neither is life in the U.S. I am guessing that paradise lies somewhere between the two extremes. For me, here, in this place, I am writing again, everyday, with a focused effort. It is my first true love and this place has renewed that part of my soul which allows me to write.

There is no certainty in life and at this moment in time, I can only hope that I will return to this blissful place. Rocco may not be in my life at that point but I can only have

155

faith in the dream that romance with someone other than myself will return soon.

I know that love gives me purpose and brings me happiness but I have also discovered that unconditional love cannot be one-sided or it ceases to nourish you and instead drains your life force.

On this trip, maybe I did not reunite with Rocco in the way that I had romanticized but I got my focus back and that is just as, if not more, important. It is what will drive me to do great things.

Piano, piano, slowly, slowly, as they say here in Italy. Relationships take time to begin, to grow, to nurture, and to mature. I am still the *straniera* here but the friends I have met I know will greet me with a cheerful smile when I return.

The *Scirocco* blows warmly today. It is a sure sign that summer has arrived.

Whoosh! The train just went by. That is the first time in two months that it sounded so loud. Maybe it is preparing me for the slap in the face which will welcome me back to the Big Apple tomorrow. I don't know what awaits me upon my return but I now know that nothing is as important as my happiness. My universe does revolve around me and for the first time I want to shout it from the top of *Vesuvio*.

A future with Rocco is no longer open for discussion with anyone but him. We will evolve together or apart and no matter what happens there is a romantic table for two, in my heart and soul, with our names forever carved into it.

Stamattina, I returned the long skeleton key and all of the keys to *La Signora*, certain she would hold them for me until my return, *a domani*.

About the Author

Lisa Fantino is an award winning journalist turned attorney. During more than 20 years at New York City's top radio news stations, WCBS-AM and WINS-AM, and as an anchor at the NBC Radio Networks, she interviewed everyone from Mick Jagger, Robert Plant and Jon Bon Jovi to Walter Cronkite, Yogi Berra and a few world leaders, along the way. Sprinkle in her liaisons with some A-list rock stars and a true romantic, wanderlust spirit and you'll understand why "fire and salsa" is the only way to describe this streetwise, sassy reporter with a Sicilian temperament. While she has traveled the world, both for work and play, Lisa's soul is always happiest in Italy. When she's not flying here, there and everywhere, her homebase is New York, where she lives on a diet of Salsa On2 and dark chocolate.

Amalfi Blue is her first book.

Visit our website at:
www.AmalfiBlueBook.com

Made in the USA
Charleston, SC
12 January 2013